THIS BOOK BELONGS TO:

CONTACT INFORMATION	
NAME:	
ADDRESS:	
PHONE:	

START / END DATES

___ / ___ / ___   TO   ___ / ___ / ___

DEDICATION

This Weekly Time Sheets Journal log is dedicated to all the hard workers out there who want to track all of their hours worked and document their findings in the process.

You are my inspiration for producing books and I'm honored to be a part of keeping all of your timesheet notes and records organized.

This journal notebook will help you record your details about your hours worked.

Thoughtfully put together with these sections to record:

Name, Department & Supervisor, Company Name, Pay Period Beginning, Date, Clock In & Out, Breaks, Daily & Total Hours, Regular & Overtime & much more!

HOW TO USE THIS BOOK

The purpose of this book is to keep all of your timesheet notes all in one place. It will help keep you organized.

This Weekly Time Sheet Journal will allow you to accurately document every detail about your hours worked. It's a great way to chart your course through recording your time spent.

Here are examples of the prompts for you to fill in and write about your experience in this book:

1. Employee Name, Address & ID Number

2. Department & Supervisor

3. Company Name, Phone Number, & Address

4. Pay Period Beginning

5. Date & Day Of The Week

6. Clock In

7. Break 1 & 2

8. Lunch

9. Clock Out

10. Daily Hours

11. Total Hours, Regular & Overtime

12. Pay Rate, Regular & Overtime

13. Total Pay, Regular & Overtime

14. Date Of Payment

15. Gross Pay

TIME SHEET

EMPLOYEE

ID NUMBER	
NAME	
ADDRESS	
DEPARTMENT	
SUPERVISOR	

COMPANY

NAME	
ADDRESS	
PHONE	
PAY PERIOD BEGINNING	

WEEK ONE

DATE	DAY OF THE WEEK	CLOCK IN	BREAK 1 BEGINS	BREAK 1 ENDS	LUNCH BEGINS	LUNCH ENDS	BREAK 2 BEGINS	BREAK 2 ENDS	CLOCK OUT	DAILY HOURS
	SUNDAY									
	MONDAY									
	TUESDAY									
	WEDNESDAY									
	THURSDAY									
	FRIDAY									
	SATURDAY									

WEEK TWO

DATE	DAY OF THE WEEK	CLOCK IN	BREAK 1 BEGINS	BREAK 1 ENDS	LUNCH BEGINS	LUNCH ENDS	BREAK 2 BEGINS	BREAK 2 ENDS	CLOCK OUT	DAILY HOURS
	SUNDAY									
	MONDAY									
	TUESDAY									
	WEDNESDAY									
	THURSDAY									
	FRIDAY									
	SATURDAY									

TOTAL HOURS | PAY RATE | TOTAL PAY

TOTAL HOURS		PAY RATE		TOTAL PAY	
REGULAR		REGULAR		REGULAR	
OVERTIME		OVERTIME		OVERTIME	

DATE OF PAYMENT			GROSS PAY	$

TIME SHEET

EMPLOYEE

ID NUMBER

NAME

ADDRESS

DEPARTMENT

SUPERVISOR

COMPANY

NAME

ADDRESS

PHONE

PAY PERIOD BEGINNING

WEEK ONE

DATE	DAY OF THE WEEK	CLOCK IN	BREAK 1 BEGINS	BREAK 1 ENDS	LUNCH BEGINS	LUNCH ENDS	BREAK 2 BEGINS	BREAK 2 ENDS	CLOCK OUT	DAILY HOURS
	SUNDAY									
	MONDAY									
	TUESDAY									
	WEDNESDAY									
	THURSDAY									
	FRIDAY									
	SATURDAY									

WEEK TWO

DATE	DAY OF THE WEEK	CLOCK IN	BREAK 1 BEGINS	BREAK 1 ENDS	LUNCH BEGINS	LUNCH ENDS	BREAK 2 BEGINS	BREAK 2 ENDS	CLOCK OUT	DAILY HOURS
	SUNDAY									
	MONDAY									
	TUESDAY									
	WEDNESDAY									
	THURSDAY									
	FRIDAY									
	SATURDAY									

TOTAL HOURS

REGULAR

OVERTIME

PAY RATE

REGULAR

OVERTIME

TOTAL PAY

REGULAR

OVERTIME

DATE OF PAYMENT

GROSS PAY $

TIME SHEET

EMPLOYEE

ID NUMBER

NAME

ADDRESS

DEPARTMENT

SUPERVISOR

COMPANY

NAME

ADDRESS

PHONE

PAY PERIOD BEGINNING

WEEK ONE

DATE	DAY OF THE WEEK	CLOCK IN	BREAK 1 BEGINS	BREAK 1 ENDS	LUNCH BEGINS	LUNCH ENDS	BREAK 2 BEGINS	BREAK 2 ENDS	CLOCK OUT	DAILY HOURS
	SUNDAY									
	MONDAY									
	TUESDAY									
	WEDNESDAY									
	THURSDAY									
	FRIDAY									
	SATURDAY									

WEEK TWO

DATE	DAY OF THE WEEK	CLOCK IN	BREAK 1 BEGINS	BREAK 1 ENDS	LUNCH BEGINS	LUNCH ENDS	BREAK 2 BEGINS	BREAK 2 ENDS	CLOCK OUT	DAILY HOURS
	SUNDAY									
	MONDAY									
	TUESDAY									
	WEDNESDAY									
	THURSDAY									
	FRIDAY									
	SATURDAY									

TOTAL HOURS   PAY RATE   TOTAL PAY

TOTAL HOURS		PAY RATE		TOTAL PAY	
REGULAR		REGULAR		REGULAR	
OVERTIME		OVERTIME		OVERTIME	

DATE OF PAYMENT			GROSS PAY	$

TIME SHEET

EMPLOYEE

ID NUMBER	
NAME	
ADDRESS	
DEPARTMENT	
SUPERVISOR	

COMPANY

NAME	
ADDRESS	
PHONE	
PAY PERIOD BEGINNING	

WEEK ONE

DATE	DAY OF THE WEEK	CLOCK IN	BREAK 1 BEGINS	BREAK 1 ENDS	LUNCH BEGINS	LUNCH ENDS	BREAK 2 BEGINS	BREAK 2 ENDS	CLOCK OUT	DAILY HOURS
	SUNDAY									
	MONDAY									
	TUESDAY									
	WEDNESDAY									
	THURSDAY									
	FRIDAY									
	SATURDAY									

WEEK TWO

DATE	DAY OF THE WEEK	CLOCK IN	BREAK 1 BEGINS	BREAK 1 ENDS	LUNCH BEGINS	LUNCH ENDS	BREAK 2 BEGINS	BREAK 2 ENDS	CLOCK OUT	DAILY HOURS
	SUNDAY									
	MONDAY									
	TUESDAY									
	WEDNESDAY									
	THURSDAY									
	FRIDAY									
	SATURDAY									

TOTAL HOURS		PAY RATE		TOTAL PAY	
REGULAR		REGULAR		REGULAR	
OVERTIME		OVERTIME		OVERTIME	
DATE OF PAYMENT				GROSS PAY	$

TIME SHEET

EMPLOYEE		COMPANY	
ID NUMBER		NAME	
NAME			
ADDRESS		ADDRESS	
DEPARTMENT		PHONE	
SUPERVISOR		PAY PERIOD BEGINNING	

WEEK ONE

DATE	DAY OF THE WEEK	CLOCK IN	BREAK 1 BEGINS	BREAK 1 ENDS	LUNCH BEGINS	LUNCH ENDS	BREAK 2 BEGINS	BREAK 2 ENDS	CLOCK OUT	DAILY HOURS
	SUNDAY									
	MONDAY									
	TUESDAY									
	WEDNESDAY									
	THURSDAY									
	FRIDAY									
	SATURDAY									

WEEK TWO

DATE	DAY OF THE WEEK	CLOCK IN	BREAK 1 BEGINS	BREAK 1 ENDS	LUNCH BEGINS	LUNCH ENDS	BREAK 2 BEGINS	BREAK 2 ENDS	CLOCK OUT	DAILY HOURS
	SUNDAY									
	MONDAY									
	TUESDAY									
	WEDNESDAY									
	THURSDAY									
	FRIDAY									
	SATURDAY									

TOTAL HOURS		PAY RATE		TOTAL PAY	
REGULAR		REGULAR		REGULAR	
OVERTIME		OVERTIME		OVERTIME	
DATE OF PAYMENT				GROSS PAY	$

TIME SHEET

EMPLOYEE

ID NUMBER

NAME

ADDRESS

DEPARTMENT

SUPERVISOR

COMPANY

NAME

ADDRESS

PHONE

PAY PERIOD BEGINNING

WEEK ONE

DATE	DAY OF THE WEEK	CLOCK IN	BREAK 1 BEGINS	BREAK 1 ENDS	LUNCH BEGINS	LUNCH ENDS	BREAK 2 BEGINS	BREAK 2 ENDS	CLOCK OUT	DAILY HOURS
	SUNDAY									
	MONDAY									
	TUESDAY									
	WEDNESDAY									
	THURSDAY									
	FRIDAY									
	SATURDAY									

WEEK TWO

DATE	DAY OF THE WEEK	CLOCK IN	BREAK 1 BEGINS	BREAK 1 ENDS	LUNCH BEGINS	LUNCH ENDS	BREAK 2 BEGINS	BREAK 2 ENDS	CLOCK OUT	DAILY HOURS
	SUNDAY									
	MONDAY									
	TUESDAY									
	WEDNESDAY									
	THURSDAY									
	FRIDAY									
	SATURDAY									

TOTAL HOURS

REGULAR

OVERTIME

PAY RATE

REGULAR

OVERTIME

TOTAL PAY

REGULAR

OVERTIME

DATE OF PAYMENT

GROSS PAY $

TIME SHEET

EMPLOYEE

ID NUMBER	
NAME	
ADDRESS	
DEPARTMENT	
SUPERVISOR	

COMPANY

NAME	
ADDRESS	
PHONE	
PAY PERIOD BEGINNING	

WEEK ONE

DATE	DAY OF THE WEEK	CLOCK IN	BREAK 1 BEGINS	BREAK 1 ENDS	LUNCH BEGINS	LUNCH ENDS	BREAK 2 BEGINS	BREAK 2 ENDS	CLOCK OUT	DAILY HOURS
	SUNDAY									
	MONDAY									
	TUESDAY									
	WEDNESDAY									
	THURSDAY									
	FRIDAY									
	SATURDAY									

WEEK TWO

DATE	DAY OF THE WEEK	CLOCK IN	BREAK 1 BEGINS	BREAK 1 ENDS	LUNCH BEGINS	LUNCH ENDS	BREAK 2 BEGINS	BREAK 2 ENDS	CLOCK OUT	DAILY HOURS
	SUNDAY									
	MONDAY									
	TUESDAY									
	WEDNESDAY									
	THURSDAY									
	FRIDAY									
	SATURDAY									

TOTAL HOURS		PAY RATE		TOTAL PAY	
REGULAR		REGULAR		REGULAR	
OVERTIME		OVERTIME		OVERTIME	
DATE OF PAYMENT				GROSS PAY	$

TIME SHEET

EMPLOYEE

ID NUMBER	
NAME	
ADDRESS	
DEPARTMENT	
SUPERVISOR	

COMPANY

NAME	
ADDRESS	
PHONE	
PAY PERIOD BEGINNING	

WEEK ONE

DATE	DAY OF THE WEEK	CLOCK IN	BREAK 1 BEGINS	BREAK 1 ENDS	LUNCH BEGINS	LUNCH ENDS	BREAK 2 BEGINS	BREAK 2 ENDS	CLOCK OUT	DAILY HOURS
	SUNDAY									
	MONDAY									
	TUESDAY									
	WEDNESDAY									
	THURSDAY									
	FRIDAY									
	SATURDAY									

WEEK TWO

DATE	DAY OF THE WEEK	CLOCK IN	BREAK 1 BEGINS	BREAK 1 ENDS	LUNCH BEGINS	LUNCH ENDS	BREAK 2 BEGINS	BREAK 2 ENDS	CLOCK OUT	DAILY HOURS
	SUNDAY									
	MONDAY									
	TUESDAY									
	WEDNESDAY									
	THURSDAY									
	FRIDAY									
	SATURDAY									

TOTAL HOURS		PAY RATE		TOTAL PAY	
REGULAR		REGULAR		REGULAR	
OVERTIME		OVERTIME		OVERTIME	
DATE OF PAYMENT				GROSS PAY	$

TIME SHEET

EMPLOYEE

ID NUMBER	
NAME	
ADDRESS	
DEPARTMENT	
SUPERVISOR	

COMPANY

NAME	
ADDRESS	
PHONE	
PAY PERIOD BEGINNING	

WEEK ONE

DATE	DAY OF THE WEEK	CLOCK IN	BREAK 1 BEGINS	BREAK 1 ENDS	LUNCH BEGINS	LUNCH ENDS	BREAK 2 BEGINS	BREAK 2 ENDS	CLOCK OUT	DAILY HOURS
	SUNDAY									
	MONDAY									
	TUESDAY									
	WEDNESDAY									
	THURSDAY									
	FRIDAY									
	SATURDAY									

WEEK TWO

DATE	DAY OF THE WEEK	CLOCK IN	BREAK 1 BEGINS	BREAK 1 ENDS	LUNCH BEGINS	LUNCH ENDS	BREAK 2 BEGINS	BREAK 2 ENDS	CLOCK OUT	DAILY HOURS
	SUNDAY									
	MONDAY									
	TUESDAY									
	WEDNESDAY									
	THURSDAY									
	FRIDAY									
	SATURDAY									

TOTAL HOURS | PAY RATE | TOTAL PAY

TOTAL HOURS		PAY RATE		TOTAL PAY	
REGULAR		REGULAR		REGULAR	
OVERTIME		OVERTIME		OVERTIME	

DATE OF PAYMENT		GROSS PAY	$

TIME SHEET

EMPLOYEE

ID NUMBER

NAME

ADDRESS

DEPARTMENT

SUPERVISOR

COMPANY

NAME

ADDRESS

PHONE

PAY PERIOD BEGINNING

WEEK ONE

DATE	DAY OF THE WEEK	CLOCK IN	BREAK 1 BEGINS	BREAK 1 ENDS	LUNCH BEGINS	LUNCH ENDS	BREAK 2 BEGINS	BREAK 2 ENDS	CLOCK OUT	DAILY HOURS
	SUNDAY									
	MONDAY									
	TUESDAY									
	WEDNESDAY									
	THURSDAY									
	FRIDAY									
	SATURDAY									

WEEK TWO

DATE	DAY OF THE WEEK	CLOCK IN	BREAK 1 BEGINS	BREAK 1 ENDS	LUNCH BEGINS	LUNCH ENDS	BREAK 2 BEGINS	BREAK 2 ENDS	CLOCK OUT	DAILY HOURS
	SUNDAY									
	MONDAY									
	TUESDAY									
	WEDNESDAY									
	THURSDAY									
	FRIDAY									
	SATURDAY									

TOTAL HOURS

REGULAR

OVERTIME

PAY RATE

REGULAR

OVERTIME

TOTAL PAY

REGULAR

OVERTIME

DATE OF PAYMENT

GROSS PAY $

TIME SHEET

EMPLOYEE

ID NUMBER	
NAME	
ADDRESS	
DEPARTMENT	
SUPERVISOR	

COMPANY

NAME	
ADDRESS	
PHONE	
PAY PERIOD BEGINNING	

WEEK ONE

DATE	DAY OF THE WEEK	CLOCK IN	BREAK 1 BEGINS	BREAK 1 ENDS	LUNCH BEGINS	LUNCH ENDS	BREAK 2 BEGINS	BREAK 2 ENDS	CLOCK OUT	DAILY HOURS
	SUNDAY									
	MONDAY									
	TUESDAY									
	WEDNESDAY									
	THURSDAY									
	FRIDAY									
	SATURDAY									

WEEK TWO

DATE	DAY OF THE WEEK	CLOCK IN	BREAK 1 BEGINS	BREAK 1 ENDS	LUNCH BEGINS	LUNCH ENDS	BREAK 2 BEGINS	BREAK 2 ENDS	CLOCK OUT	DAILY HOURS
	SUNDAY									
	MONDAY									
	TUESDAY									
	WEDNESDAY									
	THURSDAY									
	FRIDAY									
	SATURDAY									

TOTAL HOURS		PAY RATE		TOTAL PAY	
REGULAR		REGULAR		REGULAR	
OVERTIME		OVERTIME		OVERTIME	

DATE OF PAYMENT			GROSS PAY	$

TIME SHEET

EMPLOYEE

ID NUMBER

NAME

ADDRESS

DEPARTMENT

SUPERVISOR

COMPANY

NAME

ADDRESS

PHONE

PAY PERIOD BEGINNING

WEEK ONE

DATE	DAY OF THE WEEK	CLOCK IN	BREAK 1 BEGINS	BREAK 1 ENDS	LUNCH BEGINS	LUNCH ENDS	BREAK 2 BEGINS	BREAK 2 ENDS	CLOCK OUT	DAILY HOURS
	SUNDAY									
	MONDAY									
	TUESDAY									
	WEDNESDAY									
	THURSDAY									
	FRIDAY									
	SATURDAY									

WEEK TWO

DATE	DAY OF THE WEEK	CLOCK IN	BREAK 1 BEGINS	BREAK 1 ENDS	LUNCH BEGINS	LUNCH ENDS	BREAK 2 BEGINS	BREAK 2 ENDS	CLOCK OUT	DAILY HOURS
	SUNDAY									
	MONDAY									
	TUESDAY									
	WEDNESDAY									
	THURSDAY									
	FRIDAY									
	SATURDAY									

TOTAL HOURS

REGULAR

OVERTIME

PAY RATE

REGULAR

OVERTIME

TOTAL PAY

REGULAR

OVERTIME

DATE OF PAYMENT

GROSS PAY $

TIME SHEET

EMPLOYEE

ID NUMBER

NAME

ADDRESS

DEPARTMENT

SUPERVISOR

COMPANY

NAME

ADDRESS

PHONE

PAY PERIOD BEGINNING

WEEK ONE

DATE	DAY OF THE WEEK	CLOCK IN	BREAK 1 BEGINS	BREAK 1 ENDS	LUNCH BEGINS	LUNCH ENDS	BREAK 2 BEGINS	BREAK 2 ENDS	CLOCK OUT	DAILY HOURS
	SUNDAY									
	MONDAY									
	TUESDAY									
	WEDNESDAY									
	THURSDAY									
	FRIDAY									
	SATURDAY									

WEEK TWO

DATE	DAY OF THE WEEK	CLOCK IN	BREAK 1 BEGINS	BREAK 1 ENDS	LUNCH BEGINS	LUNCH ENDS	BREAK 2 BEGINS	BREAK 2 ENDS	CLOCK OUT	DAILY HOURS
	SUNDAY									
	MONDAY									
	TUESDAY									
	WEDNESDAY									
	THURSDAY									
	FRIDAY									
	SATURDAY									

TOTAL HOURS | PAY RATE | TOTAL PAY

TOTAL HOURS		PAY RATE		TOTAL PAY	
REGULAR		REGULAR		REGULAR	
OVERTIME		OVERTIME		OVERTIME	

DATE OF PAYMENT			GROSS PAY	$

TIME SHEET

EMPLOYEE

ID NUMBER

NAME

ADDRESS

DEPARTMENT

SUPERVISOR

COMPANY

NAME

ADDRESS

PHONE

PAY PERIOD BEGINNING

WEEK ONE

DATE	DAY OF THE WEEK	CLOCK IN	BREAK 1 BEGINS	BREAK 1 ENDS	LUNCH BEGINS	LUNCH ENDS	BREAK 2 BEGINS	BREAK 2 ENDS	CLOCK OUT	DAILY HOURS
	SUNDAY									
	MONDAY									
	TUESDAY									
	WEDNESDAY									
	THURSDAY									
	FRIDAY									
	SATURDAY									

WEEK TWO

DATE	DAY OF THE WEEK	CLOCK IN	BREAK 1 BEGINS	BREAK 1 ENDS	LUNCH BEGINS	LUNCH ENDS	BREAK 2 BEGINS	BREAK 2 ENDS	CLOCK OUT	DAILY HOURS
	SUNDAY									
	MONDAY									
	TUESDAY									
	WEDNESDAY									
	THURSDAY									
	FRIDAY									
	SATURDAY									

TOTAL HOURS

REGULAR

OVERTIME

PAY RATE

REGULAR

OVERTIME

TOTAL PAY

REGULAR

OVERTIME

DATE OF PAYMENT

GROSS PAY $

TIME SHEET

EMPLOYEE

ID NUMBER

NAME

ADDRESS

DEPARTMENT

SUPERVISOR

COMPANY

NAME

ADDRESS

PHONE

PAY PERIOD BEGINNING

WEEK ONE

DATE	DAY OF THE WEEK	CLOCK IN	BREAK 1 BEGINS	BREAK 1 ENDS	LUNCH BEGINS	LUNCH ENDS	BREAK 2 BEGINS	BREAK 2 ENDS	CLOCK OUT	DAILY HOURS
	SUNDAY									
	MONDAY									
	TUESDAY									
	WEDNESDAY									
	THURSDAY									
	FRIDAY									
	SATURDAY									

WEEK TWO

DATE	DAY OF THE WEEK	CLOCK IN	BREAK 1 BEGINS	BREAK 1 ENDS	LUNCH BEGINS	LUNCH ENDS	BREAK 2 BEGINS	BREAK 2 ENDS	CLOCK OUT	DAILY HOURS
	SUNDAY									
	MONDAY									
	TUESDAY									
	WEDNESDAY									
	THURSDAY									
	FRIDAY									
	SATURDAY									

TOTAL HOURS		PAY RATE		TOTAL PAY	
REGULAR		REGULAR		REGULAR	
OVERTIME		OVERTIME		OVERTIME	
DATE OF PAYMENT				GROSS PAY	$

TIME SHEET

EMPLOYEE

ID NUMBER	
NAME	
ADDRESS	
DEPARTMENT	
SUPERVISOR	

COMPANY

NAME	
ADDRESS	
PHONE	
PAY PERIOD BEGINNING	

WEEK ONE

DATE	DAY OF THE WEEK	CLOCK IN	BREAK 1 BEGINS	BREAK 1 ENDS	LUNCH BEGINS	LUNCH ENDS	BREAK 2 BEGINS	BREAK 2 ENDS	CLOCK OUT	DAILY HOURS
	SUNDAY									
	MONDAY									
	TUESDAY									
	WEDNESDAY									
	THURSDAY									
	FRIDAY									
	SATURDAY									

WEEK TWO

DATE	DAY OF THE WEEK	CLOCK IN	BREAK 1 BEGINS	BREAK 1 ENDS	LUNCH BEGINS	LUNCH ENDS	BREAK 2 BEGINS	BREAK 2 ENDS	CLOCK OUT	DAILY HOURS
	SUNDAY									
	MONDAY									
	TUESDAY									
	WEDNESDAY									
	THURSDAY									
	FRIDAY									
	SATURDAY									

TOTAL HOURS		PAY RATE		TOTAL PAY	
REGULAR		REGULAR		REGULAR	
OVERTIME		OVERTIME		OVERTIME	
DATE OF PAYMENT				GROSS PAY	$

TIME SHEET

EMPLOYEE		COMPANY	
ID NUMBER		NAME	
NAME			
ADDRESS		ADDRESS	
DEPARTMENT		PHONE	
SUPERVISOR		PAY PERIOD BEGINNING	

WEEK ONE

DATE	DAY OF THE WEEK	CLOCK IN	BREAK 1 BEGINS	BREAK 1 ENDS	LUNCH BEGINS	LUNCH ENDS	BREAK 2 BEGINS	BREAK 2 ENDS	CLOCK OUT	DAILY HOURS
	SUNDAY									
	MONDAY									
	TUESDAY									
	WEDNESDAY									
	THURSDAY									
	FRIDAY									
	SATURDAY									

WEEK TWO

DATE	DAY OF THE WEEK	CLOCK IN	BREAK 1 BEGINS	BREAK 1 ENDS	LUNCH BEGINS	LUNCH ENDS	BREAK 2 BEGINS	BREAK 2 ENDS	CLOCK OUT	DAILY HOURS
	SUNDAY									
	MONDAY									
	TUESDAY									
	WEDNESDAY									
	THURSDAY									
	FRIDAY									
	SATURDAY									

TOTAL HOURS		PAY RATE		TOTAL PAY	
REGULAR		REGULAR		REGULAR	
OVERTIME		OVERTIME		OVERTIME	
DATE OF PAYMENT				GROSS PAY	$

TIME SHEET

EMPLOYEE

ID NUMBER

NAME

ADDRESS

DEPARTMENT

SUPERVISOR

COMPANY

NAME

ADDRESS

PHONE

PAY PERIOD BEGINNING

WEEK ONE

DATE	DAY OF THE WEEK	CLOCK IN	BREAK 1 BEGINS	BREAK 1 ENDS	LUNCH BEGINS	LUNCH ENDS	BREAK 2 BEGINS	BREAK 2 ENDS	CLOCK OUT	DAILY HOURS
	SUNDAY									
	MONDAY									
	TUESDAY									
	WEDNESDAY									
	THURSDAY									
	FRIDAY									
	SATURDAY									

WEEK TWO

DATE	DAY OF THE WEEK	CLOCK IN	BREAK 1 BEGINS	BREAK 1 ENDS	LUNCH BEGINS	LUNCH ENDS	BREAK 2 BEGINS	BREAK 2 ENDS	CLOCK OUT	DAILY HOURS
	SUNDAY									
	MONDAY									
	TUESDAY									
	WEDNESDAY									
	THURSDAY									
	FRIDAY									
	SATURDAY									

TOTAL HOURS
REGULAR

OVERTIME

PAY RATE
REGULAR

OVERTIME

TOTAL PAY
REGULAR

OVERTIME

DATE OF PAYMENT

GROSS PAY $

TIME SHEET

EMPLOYEE

ID NUMBER

NAME

ADDRESS

DEPARTMENT

SUPERVISOR

COMPANY

NAME

ADDRESS

PHONE

PAY PERIOD BEGINNING

WEEK ONE

DATE	DAY OF THE WEEK	CLOCK IN	BREAK 1 BEGINS	BREAK 1 ENDS	LUNCH BEGINS	LUNCH ENDS	BREAK 2 BEGINS	BREAK 2 ENDS	CLOCK OUT	DAILY HOURS
	SUNDAY									
	MONDAY									
	TUESDAY									
	WEDNESDAY									
	THURSDAY									
	FRIDAY									
	SATURDAY									

WEEK TWO

DATE	DAY OF THE WEEK	CLOCK IN	BREAK 1 BEGINS	BREAK 1 ENDS	LUNCH BEGINS	LUNCH ENDS	BREAK 2 BEGINS	BREAK 2 ENDS	CLOCK OUT	DAILY HOURS
	SUNDAY									
	MONDAY									
	TUESDAY									
	WEDNESDAY									
	THURSDAY									
	FRIDAY									
	SATURDAY									

TOTAL HOURS		PAY RATE		TOTAL PAY	
REGULAR		REGULAR		REGULAR	
OVERTIME		OVERTIME		OVERTIME	
DATE OF PAYMENT				**GROSS PAY**	$

TIME SHEET

EMPLOYEE

ID NUMBER

NAME

ADDRESS

DEPARTMENT

SUPERVISOR

COMPANY

NAME

ADDRESS

PHONE

PAY PERIOD BEGINNING

WEEK ONE

DATE	DAY OF THE WEEK	CLOCK IN	BREAK 1 BEGINS	BREAK 1 ENDS	LUNCH BEGINS	LUNCH ENDS	BREAK 2 BEGINS	BREAK 2 ENDS	CLOCK OUT	DAILY HOURS
	SUNDAY									
	MONDAY									
	TUESDAY									
	WEDNESDAY									
	THURSDAY									
	FRIDAY									
	SATURDAY									

WEEK TWO

DATE	DAY OF THE WEEK	CLOCK IN	BREAK 1 BEGINS	BREAK 1 ENDS	LUNCH BEGINS	LUNCH ENDS	BREAK 2 BEGINS	BREAK 2 ENDS	CLOCK OUT	DAILY HOURS
	SUNDAY									
	MONDAY									
	TUESDAY									
	WEDNESDAY									
	THURSDAY									
	FRIDAY									
	SATURDAY									

TOTAL HOURS		PAY RATE		TOTAL PAY	
REGULAR		REGULAR		REGULAR	
OVERTIME		OVERTIME		OVERTIME	
DATE OF PAYMENT				GROSS PAY	$

TIME SHEET

EMPLOYEE

ID NUMBER	
NAME	
ADDRESS	
DEPARTMENT	
SUPERVISOR	

COMPANY

NAME	
ADDRESS	
PHONE	
PAY PERIOD BEGINNING	

WEEK ONE

DATE	DAY OF THE WEEK	CLOCK IN	BREAK 1 BEGINS	BREAK 1 ENDS	LUNCH BEGINS	LUNCH ENDS	BREAK 2 BEGINS	BREAK 2 ENDS	CLOCK OUT	DAILY HOURS
	SUNDAY									
	MONDAY									
	TUESDAY									
	WEDNESDAY									
	THURSDAY									
	FRIDAY									
	SATURDAY									

WEEK TWO

DATE	DAY OF THE WEEK	CLOCK IN	BREAK 1 BEGINS	BREAK 1 ENDS	LUNCH BEGINS	LUNCH ENDS	BREAK 2 BEGINS	BREAK 2 ENDS	CLOCK OUT	DAILY HOURS
	SUNDAY									
	MONDAY									
	TUESDAY									
	WEDNESDAY									
	THURSDAY									
	FRIDAY									
	SATURDAY									

TOTAL HOURS		PAY RATE		TOTAL PAY	
REGULAR		REGULAR		REGULAR	
OVERTIME		OVERTIME		OVERTIME	
DATE OF PAYMENT				GROSS PAY	$

TIME SHEET

EMPLOYEE

ID NUMBER	
NAME	
ADDRESS	
DEPARTMENT	
SUPERVISOR	

COMPANY

NAME	
ADDRESS	
PHONE	
PAY PERIOD BEGINNING	

WEEK ONE

DATE	DAY OF THE WEEK	CLOCK IN	BREAK 1 BEGINS	BREAK 1 ENDS	LUNCH BEGINS	LUNCH ENDS	BREAK 2 BEGINS	BREAK 2 ENDS	CLOCK OUT	DAILY HOURS
	SUNDAY									
	MONDAY									
	TUESDAY									
	WEDNESDAY									
	THURSDAY									
	FRIDAY									
	SATURDAY									

WEEK TWO

DATE	DAY OF THE WEEK	CLOCK IN	BREAK 1 BEGINS	BREAK 1 ENDS	LUNCH BEGINS	LUNCH ENDS	BREAK 2 BEGINS	BREAK 2 ENDS	CLOCK OUT	DAILY HOURS
	SUNDAY									
	MONDAY									
	TUESDAY									
	WEDNESDAY									
	THURSDAY									
	FRIDAY									
	SATURDAY									

TOTAL HOURS

REGULAR	
OVERTIME	

PAY RATE

REGULAR	
OVERTIME	

TOTAL PAY

REGULAR	
OVERTIME	

DATE OF PAYMENT		GROSS PAY	$

TIME SHEET

EMPLOYEE

ID NUMBER	
NAME	
ADDRESS	
DEPARTMENT	
SUPERVISOR	

COMPANY

NAME	
ADDRESS	
PHONE	
PAY PERIOD BEGINNING	

WEEK ONE

DATE	DAY OF THE WEEK	CLOCK IN	BREAK 1 BEGINS	BREAK 1 ENDS	LUNCH BEGINS	LUNCH ENDS	BREAK 2 BEGINS	BREAK 2 ENDS	CLOCK OUT	DAILY HOURS
	SUNDAY									
	MONDAY									
	TUESDAY									
	WEDNESDAY									
	THURSDAY									
	FRIDAY									
	SATURDAY									

WEEK TWO

DATE	DAY OF THE WEEK	CLOCK IN	BREAK 1 BEGINS	BREAK 1 ENDS	LUNCH BEGINS	LUNCH ENDS	BREAK 2 BEGINS	BREAK 2 ENDS	CLOCK OUT	DAILY HOURS
	SUNDAY									
	MONDAY									
	TUESDAY									
	WEDNESDAY									
	THURSDAY									
	FRIDAY									
	SATURDAY									

TOTAL HOURS | PAY RATE | TOTAL PAY

TOTAL HOURS		PAY RATE		TOTAL PAY	
REGULAR		REGULAR		REGULAR	
OVERTIME		OVERTIME		OVERTIME	

DATE OF PAYMENT			GROSS PAY	$

TIME SHEET

EMPLOYEE

ID NUMBER

NAME

ADDRESS

DEPARTMENT

SUPERVISOR

COMPANY

NAME

ADDRESS

PHONE

PAY PERIOD BEGINNING

WEEK ONE

DATE	DAY OF THE WEEK	CLOCK IN	BREAK 1 BEGINS	BREAK 1 ENDS	LUNCH BEGINS	LUNCH ENDS	BREAK 2 BEGINS	BREAK 2 ENDS	CLOCK OUT	DAILY HOURS
	SUNDAY									
	MONDAY									
	TUESDAY									
	WEDNESDAY									
	THURSDAY									
	FRIDAY									
	SATURDAY									

WEEK TWO

DATE	DAY OF THE WEEK	CLOCK IN	BREAK 1 BEGINS	BREAK 1 ENDS	LUNCH BEGINS	LUNCH ENDS	BREAK 2 BEGINS	BREAK 2 ENDS	CLOCK OUT	DAILY HOURS
	SUNDAY									
	MONDAY									
	TUESDAY									
	WEDNESDAY									
	THURSDAY									
	FRIDAY									
	SATURDAY									

TOTAL HOURS

REGULAR

OVERTIME

PAY RATE

REGULAR

OVERTIME

TOTAL PAY

REGULAR

OVERTIME

DATE OF PAYMENT

GROSS PAY $

TIME SHEET

EMPLOYEE		COMPANY	
ID NUMBER		NAME	
NAME			
ADDRESS		ADDRESS	
DEPARTMENT		PHONE	
SUPERVISOR		PAY PERIOD BEGINNING	

WEEK ONE

DATE	DAY OF THE WEEK	CLOCK IN	BREAK 1 BEGINS	BREAK 1 ENDS	LUNCH BEGINS	LUNCH ENDS	BREAK 2 BEGINS	BREAK 2 ENDS	CLOCK OUT	DAILY HOURS
	SUNDAY									
	MONDAY									
	TUESDAY									
	WEDNESDAY									
	THURSDAY									
	FRIDAY									
	SATURDAY									

WEEK TWO

DATE	DAY OF THE WEEK	CLOCK IN	BREAK 1 BEGINS	BREAK 1 ENDS	LUNCH BEGINS	LUNCH ENDS	BREAK 2 BEGINS	BREAK 2 ENDS	CLOCK OUT	DAILY HOURS
	SUNDAY									
	MONDAY									
	TUESDAY									
	WEDNESDAY									
	THURSDAY									
	FRIDAY									
	SATURDAY									

TOTAL HOURS		PAY RATE		TOTAL PAY	
REGULAR		REGULAR		REGULAR	
OVERTIME		OVERTIME		OVERTIME	
DATE OF PAYMENT				GROSS PAY	$

TIME SHEET

EMPLOYEE

ID NUMBER

NAME

ADDRESS

DEPARTMENT

SUPERVISOR

COMPANY

NAME

ADDRESS

PHONE

PAY PERIOD BEGINNING

WEEK ONE

DATE	DAY OF THE WEEK	CLOCK IN	BREAK 1 BEGINS	BREAK 1 ENDS	LUNCH BEGINS	LUNCH ENDS	BREAK 2 BEGINS	BREAK 2 ENDS	CLOCK OUT	DAILY HOURS
	SUNDAY									
	MONDAY									
	TUESDAY									
	WEDNESDAY									
	THURSDAY									
	FRIDAY									
	SATURDAY									

WEEK TWO

DATE	DAY OF THE WEEK	CLOCK IN	BREAK 1 BEGINS	BREAK 1 ENDS	LUNCH BEGINS	LUNCH ENDS	BREAK 2 BEGINS	BREAK 2 ENDS	CLOCK OUT	DAILY HOURS
	SUNDAY									
	MONDAY									
	TUESDAY									
	WEDNESDAY									
	THURSDAY									
	FRIDAY									
	SATURDAY									

TOTAL HOURS

REGULAR

OVERTIME

PAY RATE

REGULAR

OVERTIME

TOTAL PAY

REGULAR

OVERTIME

DATE OF PAYMENT

GROSS PAY $

TIME SHEET

EMPLOYEE

ID NUMBER	
NAME	
ADDRESS	
DEPARTMENT	
SUPERVISOR	

COMPANY

NAME	
ADDRESS	
PHONE	
PAY PERIOD BEGINNING	

WEEK ONE

DATE	DAY OF THE WEEK	CLOCK IN	BREAK 1 BEGINS	BREAK 1 ENDS	LUNCH BEGINS	LUNCH ENDS	BREAK 2 BEGINS	BREAK 2 ENDS	CLOCK OUT	DAILY HOURS
	SUNDAY									
	MONDAY									
	TUESDAY									
	WEDNESDAY									
	THURSDAY									
	FRIDAY									
	SATURDAY									

WEEK TWO

DATE	DAY OF THE WEEK	CLOCK IN	BREAK 1 BEGINS	BREAK 1 ENDS	LUNCH BEGINS	LUNCH ENDS	BREAK 2 BEGINS	BREAK 2 ENDS	CLOCK OUT	DAILY HOURS
	SUNDAY									
	MONDAY									
	TUESDAY									
	WEDNESDAY									
	THURSDAY									
	FRIDAY									
	SATURDAY									

TOTAL HOURS		PAY RATE		TOTAL PAY	
REGULAR		REGULAR		REGULAR	
OVERTIME		OVERTIME		OVERTIME	
DATE OF PAYMENT				GROSS PAY	$

TIME SHEET

EMPLOYEE

ID NUMBER

NAME

ADDRESS

DEPARTMENT

SUPERVISOR

COMPANY

NAME

ADDRESS

PHONE

PAY PERIOD BEGINNING

WEEK ONE

DATE	DAY OF THE WEEK	CLOCK IN	BREAK 1 BEGINS	BREAK 1 ENDS	LUNCH BEGINS	LUNCH ENDS	BREAK 2 BEGINS	BREAK 2 ENDS	CLOCK OUT	DAILY HOURS
	SUNDAY									
	MONDAY									
	TUESDAY									
	WEDNESDAY									
	THURSDAY									
	FRIDAY									
	SATURDAY									

WEEK TWO

DATE	DAY OF THE WEEK	CLOCK IN	BREAK 1 BEGINS	BREAK 1 ENDS	LUNCH BEGINS	LUNCH ENDS	BREAK 2 BEGINS	BREAK 2 ENDS	CLOCK OUT	DAILY HOURS
	SUNDAY									
	MONDAY									
	TUESDAY									
	WEDNESDAY									
	THURSDAY									
	FRIDAY									
	SATURDAY									

TOTAL HOURS		PAY RATE		TOTAL PAY	
REGULAR		REGULAR		REGULAR	
OVERTIME		OVERTIME		OVERTIME	
DATE OF PAYMENT				GROSS PAY	$

TIME SHEET

EMPLOYEE

ID NUMBER	
NAME	
ADDRESS	
DEPARTMENT	
SUPERVISOR	

COMPANY

NAME	
ADDRESS	
PHONE	
PAY PERIOD BEGINNING	

WEEK ONE

DATE	DAY OF THE WEEK	CLOCK IN	BREAK 1 BEGINS	BREAK 1 ENDS	LUNCH BEGINS	LUNCH ENDS	BREAK 2 BEGINS	BREAK 2 ENDS	CLOCK OUT	DAILY HOURS
	SUNDAY									
	MONDAY									
	TUESDAY									
	WEDNESDAY									
	THURSDAY									
	FRIDAY									
	SATURDAY									

WEEK TWO

DATE	DAY OF THE WEEK	CLOCK IN	BREAK 1 BEGINS	BREAK 1 ENDS	LUNCH BEGINS	LUNCH ENDS	BREAK 2 BEGINS	BREAK 2 ENDS	CLOCK OUT	DAILY HOURS
	SUNDAY									
	MONDAY									
	TUESDAY									
	WEDNESDAY									
	THURSDAY									
	FRIDAY									
	SATURDAY									

TOTAL HOURS		PAY RATE		TOTAL PAY	
REGULAR		REGULAR		REGULAR	
OVERTIME		OVERTIME		OVERTIME	

DATE OF PAYMENT		GROSS PAY	$

TIME SHEET

EMPLOYEE

ID NUMBER

NAME

ADDRESS

DEPARTMENT

SUPERVISOR

COMPANY

NAME

ADDRESS

PHONE

PAY PERIOD BEGINNING

WEEK ONE

DATE	DAY OF THE WEEK	CLOCK IN	BREAK 1 BEGINS	BREAK 1 ENDS	LUNCH BEGINS	LUNCH ENDS	BREAK 2 BEGINS	BREAK 2 ENDS	CLOCK OUT	DAILY HOURS
	SUNDAY									
	MONDAY									
	TUESDAY									
	WEDNESDAY									
	THURSDAY									
	FRIDAY									
	SATURDAY									

WEEK TWO

DATE	DAY OF THE WEEK	CLOCK IN	BREAK 1 BEGINS	BREAK 1 ENDS	LUNCH BEGINS	LUNCH ENDS	BREAK 2 BEGINS	BREAK 2 ENDS	CLOCK OUT	DAILY HOURS
	SUNDAY									
	MONDAY									
	TUESDAY									
	WEDNESDAY									
	THURSDAY									
	FRIDAY									
	SATURDAY									

TOTAL HOURS		PAY RATE		TOTAL PAY	
REGULAR		REGULAR		REGULAR	
OVERTIME		OVERTIME		OVERTIME	
DATE OF PAYMENT				GROSS PAY	$

TIME SHEET

EMPLOYEE

ID NUMBER	
NAME	
ADDRESS	
DEPARTMENT	
SUPERVISOR	

COMPANY

NAME	
ADDRESS	
PHONE	
PAY PERIOD BEGINNING	

WEEK ONE

DATE	DAY OF THE WEEK	CLOCK IN	BREAK 1 BEGINS	BREAK 1 ENDS	LUNCH BEGINS	LUNCH ENDS	BREAK 2 BEGINS	BREAK 2 ENDS	CLOCK OUT	DAILY HOURS
	SUNDAY									
	MONDAY									
	TUESDAY									
	WEDNESDAY									
	THURSDAY									
	FRIDAY									
	SATURDAY									

WEEK TWO

DATE	DAY OF THE WEEK	CLOCK IN	BREAK 1 BEGINS	BREAK 1 ENDS	LUNCH BEGINS	LUNCH ENDS	BREAK 2 BEGINS	BREAK 2 ENDS	CLOCK OUT	DAILY HOURS
	SUNDAY									
	MONDAY									
	TUESDAY									
	WEDNESDAY									
	THURSDAY									
	FRIDAY									
	SATURDAY									

TOTAL HOURS		PAY RATE		TOTAL PAY	
REGULAR		REGULAR		REGULAR	
OVERTIME		OVERTIME		OVERTIME	

DATE OF PAYMENT			GROSS PAY	$

TIME SHEET

EMPLOYEE

ID NUMBER

NAME

ADDRESS

DEPARTMENT

SUPERVISOR

COMPANY

NAME

ADDRESS

PHONE

PAY PERIOD BEGINNING

WEEK ONE

DATE	DAY OF THE WEEK	CLOCK IN	BREAK 1 BEGINS	BREAK 1 ENDS	LUNCH BEGINS	LUNCH ENDS	BREAK 2 BEGINS	BREAK 2 ENDS	CLOCK OUT	DAILY HOURS
	SUNDAY									
	MONDAY									
	TUESDAY									
	WEDNESDAY									
	THURSDAY									
	FRIDAY									
	SATURDAY									

WEEK TWO

DATE	DAY OF THE WEEK	CLOCK IN	BREAK 1 BEGINS	BREAK 1 ENDS	LUNCH BEGINS	LUNCH ENDS	BREAK 2 BEGINS	BREAK 2 ENDS	CLOCK OUT	DAILY HOURS
	SUNDAY									
	MONDAY									
	TUESDAY									
	WEDNESDAY									
	THURSDAY									
	FRIDAY									
	SATURDAY									

TOTAL HOURS

REGULAR

OVERTIME

PAY RATE

REGULAR

OVERTIME

TOTAL PAY

REGULAR

OVERTIME

DATE OF PAYMENT

GROSS PAY $

TIME SHEET

EMPLOYEE

ID NUMBER	
NAME	
ADDRESS	
DEPARTMENT	
SUPERVISOR	

COMPANY

NAME	
ADDRESS	
PHONE	
PAY PERIOD BEGINNING	

WEEK ONE

DATE	DAY OF THE WEEK	CLOCK IN	BREAK 1 BEGINS	BREAK 1 ENDS	LUNCH BEGINS	LUNCH ENDS	BREAK 2 BEGINS	BREAK 2 ENDS	CLOCK OUT	DAILY HOURS
	SUNDAY									
	MONDAY									
	TUESDAY									
	WEDNESDAY									
	THURSDAY									
	FRIDAY									
	SATURDAY									

WEEK TWO

DATE	DAY OF THE WEEK	CLOCK IN	BREAK 1 BEGINS	BREAK 1 ENDS	LUNCH BEGINS	LUNCH ENDS	BREAK 2 BEGINS	BREAK 2 ENDS	CLOCK OUT	DAILY HOURS
	SUNDAY									
	MONDAY									
	TUESDAY									
	WEDNESDAY									
	THURSDAY									
	FRIDAY									
	SATURDAY									

TOTAL HOURS		PAY RATE		TOTAL PAY	
REGULAR		REGULAR		REGULAR	
OVERTIME		OVERTIME		OVERTIME	
DATE OF PAYMENT				GROSS PAY	$

TIME SHEET

EMPLOYEE

ID NUMBER

NAME

ADDRESS

DEPARTMENT

SUPERVISOR

COMPANY

NAME

ADDRESS

PHONE

PAY PERIOD BEGINNING

WEEK ONE

DATE	DAY OF THE WEEK	CLOCK IN	BREAK 1 BEGINS	BREAK 1 ENDS	LUNCH BEGINS	LUNCH ENDS	BREAK 2 BEGINS	BREAK 2 ENDS	CLOCK OUT	DAILY HOURS
	SUNDAY									
	MONDAY									
	TUESDAY									
	WEDNESDAY									
	THURSDAY									
	FRIDAY									
	SATURDAY									

WEEK TWO

DATE	DAY OF THE WEEK	CLOCK IN	BREAK 1 BEGINS	BREAK 1 ENDS	LUNCH BEGINS	LUNCH ENDS	BREAK 2 BEGINS	BREAK 2 ENDS	CLOCK OUT	DAILY HOURS
	SUNDAY									
	MONDAY									
	TUESDAY									
	WEDNESDAY									
	THURSDAY									
	FRIDAY									
	SATURDAY									

TOTAL HOURS

REGULAR

OVERTIME

PAY RATE

REGULAR

OVERTIME

TOTAL PAY

REGULAR

OVERTIME

DATE OF PAYMENT

GROSS PAY $

TIME SHEET

EMPLOYEE

ID NUMBER

NAME

ADDRESS

DEPARTMENT

SUPERVISOR

COMPANY

NAME

ADDRESS

PHONE

PAY PERIOD BEGINNING

WEEK ONE

DATE	DAY OF THE WEEK	CLOCK IN	BREAK 1 BEGINS	BREAK 1 ENDS	LUNCH BEGINS	LUNCH ENDS	BREAK 2 BEGINS	BREAK 2 ENDS	CLOCK OUT	DAILY HOURS
	SUNDAY									
	MONDAY									
	TUESDAY									
	WEDNESDAY									
	THURSDAY									
	FRIDAY									
	SATURDAY									

WEEK TWO

DATE	DAY OF THE WEEK	CLOCK IN	BREAK 1 BEGINS	BREAK 1 ENDS	LUNCH BEGINS	LUNCH ENDS	BREAK 2 BEGINS	BREAK 2 ENDS	CLOCK OUT	DAILY HOURS
	SUNDAY									
	MONDAY									
	TUESDAY									
	WEDNESDAY									
	THURSDAY									
	FRIDAY									
	SATURDAY									

TOTAL HOURS		PAY RATE		TOTAL PAY	
REGULAR		REGULAR		REGULAR	
OVERTIME		OVERTIME		OVERTIME	

DATE OF PAYMENT		GROSS PAY	$

TIME SHEET

EMPLOYEE

ID NUMBER

NAME

ADDRESS

DEPARTMENT

SUPERVISOR

COMPANY

NAME

ADDRESS

PHONE

PAY PERIOD BEGINNING

WEEK ONE

DATE	DAY OF THE WEEK	CLOCK IN	BREAK 1 BEGINS	BREAK 1 ENDS	LUNCH BEGINS	LUNCH ENDS	BREAK 2 BEGINS	BREAK 2 ENDS	CLOCK OUT	DAILY HOURS
	SUNDAY									
	MONDAY									
	TUESDAY									
	WEDNESDAY									
	THURSDAY									
	FRIDAY									
	SATURDAY									

WEEK TWO

DATE	DAY OF THE WEEK	CLOCK IN	BREAK 1 BEGINS	BREAK 1 ENDS	LUNCH BEGINS	LUNCH ENDS	BREAK 2 BEGINS	BREAK 2 ENDS	CLOCK OUT	DAILY HOURS
	SUNDAY									
	MONDAY									
	TUESDAY									
	WEDNESDAY									
	THURSDAY									
	FRIDAY									
	SATURDAY									

TOTAL HOURS		PAY RATE		TOTAL PAY	
REGULAR		REGULAR		REGULAR	
OVERTIME		OVERTIME		OVERTIME	

DATE OF PAYMENT		GROSS PAY	$

TIME SHEET

EMPLOYEE

ID NUMBER

NAME

ADDRESS

DEPARTMENT

SUPERVISOR

COMPANY

NAME

ADDRESS

PHONE

PAY PERIOD BEGINNING

WEEK ONE

DATE	DAY OF THE WEEK	CLOCK IN	BREAK 1 BEGINS	BREAK 1 ENDS	LUNCH BEGINS	LUNCH ENDS	BREAK 2 BEGINS	BREAK 2 ENDS	CLOCK OUT	DAILY HOURS
	SUNDAY									
	MONDAY									
	TUESDAY									
	WEDNESDAY									
	THURSDAY									
	FRIDAY									
	SATURDAY									

WEEK TWO

DATE	DAY OF THE WEEK	CLOCK IN	BREAK 1 BEGINS	BREAK 1 ENDS	LUNCH BEGINS	LUNCH ENDS	BREAK 2 BEGINS	BREAK 2 ENDS	CLOCK OUT	DAILY HOURS
	SUNDAY									
	MONDAY									
	TUESDAY									
	WEDNESDAY									
	THURSDAY									
	FRIDAY									
	SATURDAY									

TOTAL HOURS		PAY RATE		TOTAL PAY	
REGULAR		REGULAR		REGULAR	
OVERTIME		OVERTIME		OVERTIME	

DATE OF PAYMENT			GROSS PAY	$

TIME SHEET

EMPLOYEE

ID NUMBER

NAME

ADDRESS

DEPARTMENT

SUPERVISOR

COMPANY

NAME

ADDRESS

PHONE

PAY PERIOD BEGINNING

WEEK ONE

DATE	DAY OF THE WEEK	CLOCK IN	BREAK 1 BEGINS	BREAK 1 ENDS	LUNCH BEGINS	LUNCH ENDS	BREAK 2 BEGINS	BREAK 2 ENDS	CLOCK OUT	DAILY HOURS
	SUNDAY									
	MONDAY									
	TUESDAY									
	WEDNESDAY									
	THURSDAY									
	FRIDAY									
	SATURDAY									

WEEK TWO

DATE	DAY OF THE WEEK	CLOCK IN	BREAK 1 BEGINS	BREAK 1 ENDS	LUNCH BEGINS	LUNCH ENDS	BREAK 2 BEGINS	BREAK 2 ENDS	CLOCK OUT	DAILY HOURS
	SUNDAY									
	MONDAY									
	TUESDAY									
	WEDNESDAY									
	THURSDAY									
	FRIDAY									
	SATURDAY									

TOTAL HOURS

REGULAR

OVERTIME

PAY RATE

REGULAR

OVERTIME

TOTAL PAY

REGULAR

OVERTIME

DATE OF PAYMENT

GROSS PAY $

TIME SHEET

<table>
<tr><th colspan="2">EMPLOYEE</th><th colspan="2">COMPANY</th></tr>
<tr><td>ID NUMBER</td><td></td><td>NAME</td><td></td></tr>
<tr><td>NAME</td><td></td><td></td><td></td></tr>
<tr><td>ADDRESS</td><td></td><td>ADDRESS</td><td></td></tr>
<tr><td></td><td></td><td></td><td></td></tr>
<tr><td>DEPARTMENT</td><td></td><td>PHONE</td><td></td></tr>
<tr><td>SUPERVISOR</td><td></td><td>PAY PERIOD BEGINNING</td><td></td></tr>
</table>

WEEK ONE

DATE	DAY OF THE WEEK	CLOCK IN	BREAK 1 BEGINS	BREAK 1 ENDS	LUNCH BEGINS	LUNCH ENDS	BREAK 2 BEGINS	BREAK 2 ENDS	CLOCK OUT	DAILY HOURS
	SUNDAY									
	MONDAY									
	TUESDAY									
	WEDNESDAY									
	THURSDAY									
	FRIDAY									
	SATURDAY									

WEEK TWO

DATE	DAY OF THE WEEK	CLOCK IN	BREAK 1 BEGINS	BREAK 1 ENDS	LUNCH BEGINS	LUNCH ENDS	BREAK 2 BEGINS	BREAK 2 ENDS	CLOCK OUT	DAILY HOURS
	SUNDAY									
	MONDAY									
	TUESDAY									
	WEDNESDAY									
	THURSDAY									
	FRIDAY									
	SATURDAY									

TOTAL HOURS		PAY RATE		TOTAL PAY	
REGULAR		REGULAR		REGULAR	
OVERTIME		OVERTIME		OVERTIME	

DATE OF PAYMENT			GROSS PAY	$

TIME SHEET

EMPLOYEE

ID NUMBER

NAME

ADDRESS

DEPARTMENT

SUPERVISOR

COMPANY

NAME

ADDRESS

PHONE

PAY PERIOD BEGINNING

WEEK ONE

DATE	DAY OF THE WEEK	CLOCK IN	BREAK 1 BEGINS	BREAK 1 ENDS	LUNCH BEGINS	LUNCH ENDS	BREAK 2 BEGINS	BREAK 2 ENDS	CLOCK OUT	DAILY HOURS
	SUNDAY									
	MONDAY									
	TUESDAY									
	WEDNESDAY									
	THURSDAY									
	FRIDAY									
	SATURDAY									

WEEK TWO

DATE	DAY OF THE WEEK	CLOCK IN	BREAK 1 BEGINS	BREAK 1 ENDS	LUNCH BEGINS	LUNCH ENDS	BREAK 2 BEGINS	BREAK 2 ENDS	CLOCK OUT	DAILY HOURS
	SUNDAY									
	MONDAY									
	TUESDAY									
	WEDNESDAY									
	THURSDAY									
	FRIDAY									
	SATURDAY									

TOTAL HOURS

REGULAR

OVERTIME

PAY RATE

REGULAR

OVERTIME

TOTAL PAY

REGULAR

OVERTIME

DATE OF PAYMENT

GROSS PAY $

TIME SHEET

EMPLOYEE

ID NUMBER

NAME

ADDRESS

DEPARTMENT

SUPERVISOR

COMPANY

NAME

ADDRESS

PHONE

PAY PERIOD BEGINNING

WEEK ONE

DATE	DAY OF THE WEEK	CLOCK IN	BREAK 1 BEGINS	BREAK 1 ENDS	LUNCH BEGINS	LUNCH ENDS	BREAK 2 BEGINS	BREAK 2 ENDS	CLOCK OUT	DAILY HOURS
	SUNDAY									
	MONDAY									
	TUESDAY									
	WEDNESDAY									
	THURSDAY									
	FRIDAY									
	SATURDAY									

WEEK TWO

DATE	DAY OF THE WEEK	CLOCK IN	BREAK 1 BEGINS	BREAK 1 ENDS	LUNCH BEGINS	LUNCH ENDS	BREAK 2 BEGINS	BREAK 2 ENDS	CLOCK OUT	DAILY HOURS
	SUNDAY									
	MONDAY									
	TUESDAY									
	WEDNESDAY									
	THURSDAY									
	FRIDAY									
	SATURDAY									

TOTAL HOURS | PAY RATE | TOTAL PAY

TOTAL HOURS		PAY RATE		TOTAL PAY	
REGULAR		REGULAR		REGULAR	
OVERTIME		OVERTIME		OVERTIME	

DATE OF PAYMENT		GROSS PAY	$

TIME SHEET

EMPLOYEE

ID NUMBER

NAME

ADDRESS

DEPARTMENT

SUPERVISOR

COMPANY

NAME

ADDRESS

PHONE

PAY PERIOD BEGINNING

WEEK ONE

DATE	DAY OF THE WEEK	CLOCK IN	BREAK 1 BEGINS	BREAK 1 ENDS	LUNCH BEGINS	LUNCH ENDS	BREAK 2 BEGINS	BREAK 2 ENDS	CLOCK OUT	DAILY HOURS
	SUNDAY									
	MONDAY									
	TUESDAY									
	WEDNESDAY									
	THURSDAY									
	FRIDAY									
	SATURDAY									

WEEK TWO

DATE	DAY OF THE WEEK	CLOCK IN	BREAK 1 BEGINS	BREAK 1 ENDS	LUNCH BEGINS	LUNCH ENDS	BREAK 2 BEGINS	BREAK 2 ENDS	CLOCK OUT	DAILY HOURS
	SUNDAY									
	MONDAY									
	TUESDAY									
	WEDNESDAY									
	THURSDAY									
	FRIDAY									
	SATURDAY									

TOTAL HOURS

REGULAR

OVERTIME

PAY RATE

REGULAR

OVERTIME

TOTAL PAY

REGULAR

OVERTIME

DATE OF PAYMENT

GROSS PAY $

TIME SHEET

EMPLOYEE

ID NUMBER

NAME

ADDRESS

DEPARTMENT

SUPERVISOR

COMPANY

NAME

ADDRESS

PHONE

PAY PERIOD BEGINNING

WEEK ONE

DATE	DAY OF THE WEEK	CLOCK IN	BREAK 1 BEGINS	BREAK 1 ENDS	LUNCH BEGINS	LUNCH ENDS	BREAK 2 BEGINS	BREAK 2 ENDS	CLOCK OUT	DAILY HOURS
	SUNDAY									
	MONDAY									
	TUESDAY									
	WEDNESDAY									
	THURSDAY									
	FRIDAY									
	SATURDAY									

WEEK TWO

DATE	DAY OF THE WEEK	CLOCK IN	BREAK 1 BEGINS	BREAK 1 ENDS	LUNCH BEGINS	LUNCH ENDS	BREAK 2 BEGINS	BREAK 2 ENDS	CLOCK OUT	DAILY HOURS
	SUNDAY									
	MONDAY									
	TUESDAY									
	WEDNESDAY									
	THURSDAY									
	FRIDAY									
	SATURDAY									

TOTAL HOURS

REGULAR

OVERTIME

PAY RATE

REGULAR

OVERTIME

TOTAL PAY

REGULAR

OVERTIME

DATE OF PAYMENT

GROSS PAY $

TIME SHEET

EMPLOYEE

ID NUMBER

NAME

ADDRESS

DEPARTMENT

SUPERVISOR

COMPANY

NAME

ADDRESS

PHONE

PAY PERIOD BEGINNING

WEEK ONE

DATE	DAY OF THE WEEK	CLOCK IN	BREAK 1 BEGINS	BREAK 1 ENDS	LUNCH BEGINS	LUNCH ENDS	BREAK 2 BEGINS	BREAK 2 ENDS	CLOCK OUT	DAILY HOURS
	SUNDAY									
	MONDAY									
	TUESDAY									
	WEDNESDAY									
	THURSDAY									
	FRIDAY									
	SATURDAY									

WEEK TWO

DATE	DAY OF THE WEEK	CLOCK IN	BREAK 1 BEGINS	BREAK 1 ENDS	LUNCH BEGINS	LUNCH ENDS	BREAK 2 BEGINS	BREAK 2 ENDS	CLOCK OUT	DAILY HOURS
	SUNDAY									
	MONDAY									
	TUESDAY									
	WEDNESDAY									
	THURSDAY									
	FRIDAY									
	SATURDAY									

TOTAL HOURS		PAY RATE		TOTAL PAY	
REGULAR		REGULAR		REGULAR	
OVERTIME		OVERTIME		OVERTIME	

DATE OF PAYMENT		GROSS PAY	$

TIME SHEET

<table>
<tr><td colspan="2">EMPLOYEE</td><td colspan="2">COMPANY</td></tr>
<tr><td>ID NUMBER</td><td></td><td>NAME</td><td></td></tr>
<tr><td>NAME</td><td></td><td></td><td></td></tr>
<tr><td>ADDRESS</td><td></td><td>ADDRESS</td><td></td></tr>
<tr><td>DEPARTMENT</td><td></td><td>PHONE</td><td></td></tr>
<tr><td>SUPERVISOR</td><td></td><td>PAY PERIOD BEGINNING</td><td></td></tr>
</table>

WEEK ONE

DATE	DAY OF THE WEEK	CLOCK IN	BREAK 1 BEGINS	BREAK 1 ENDS	LUNCH BEGINS	LUNCH ENDS	BREAK 2 BEGINS	BREAK 2 ENDS	CLOCK OUT	DAILY HOURS
	SUNDAY									
	MONDAY									
	TUESDAY									
	WEDNESDAY									
	THURSDAY									
	FRIDAY									
	SATURDAY									

WEEK TWO

DATE	DAY OF THE WEEK	CLOCK IN	BREAK 1 BEGINS	BREAK 1 ENDS	LUNCH BEGINS	LUNCH ENDS	BREAK 2 BEGINS	BREAK 2 ENDS	CLOCK OUT	DAILY HOURS
	SUNDAY									
	MONDAY									
	TUESDAY									
	WEDNESDAY									
	THURSDAY									
	FRIDAY									
	SATURDAY									

TOTAL HOURS		PAY RATE		TOTAL PAY	
REGULAR		REGULAR		REGULAR	
OVERTIME		OVERTIME		OVERTIME	
DATE OF PAYMENT				GROSS PAY	$

TIME SHEET

EMPLOYEE

ID NUMBER

NAME

ADDRESS

DEPARTMENT

SUPERVISOR

COMPANY

NAME

ADDRESS

PHONE

PAY PERIOD BEGINNING

WEEK ONE

DATE	DAY OF THE WEEK	CLOCK IN	BREAK 1 BEGINS	BREAK 1 ENDS	LUNCH BEGINS	LUNCH ENDS	BREAK 2 BEGINS	BREAK 2 ENDS	CLOCK OUT	DAILY HOURS
	SUNDAY									
	MONDAY									
	TUESDAY									
	WEDNESDAY									
	THURSDAY									
	FRIDAY									
	SATURDAY									

WEEK TWO

DATE	DAY OF THE WEEK	CLOCK IN	BREAK 1 BEGINS	BREAK 1 ENDS	LUNCH BEGINS	LUNCH ENDS	BREAK 2 BEGINS	BREAK 2 ENDS	CLOCK OUT	DAILY HOURS
	SUNDAY									
	MONDAY									
	TUESDAY									
	WEDNESDAY									
	THURSDAY									
	FRIDAY									
	SATURDAY									

TOTAL HOURS		PAY RATE		TOTAL PAY	
REGULAR		REGULAR		REGULAR	
OVERTIME		OVERTIME		OVERTIME	

DATE OF PAYMENT		GROSS PAY $

TIME SHEET

EMPLOYEE

ID NUMBER

NAME

ADDRESS

DEPARTMENT

SUPERVISOR

COMPANY

NAME

ADDRESS

PHONE

PAY PERIOD BEGINNING

WEEK ONE

DATE	DAY OF THE WEEK	CLOCK IN	BREAK 1 BEGINS	BREAK 1 ENDS	LUNCH BEGINS	LUNCH ENDS	BREAK 2 BEGINS	BREAK 2 ENDS	CLOCK OUT	DAILY HOURS
	SUNDAY									
	MONDAY									
	TUESDAY									
	WEDNESDAY									
	THURSDAY									
	FRIDAY									
	SATURDAY									

WEEK TWO

DATE	DAY OF THE WEEK	CLOCK IN	BREAK 1 BEGINS	BREAK 1 ENDS	LUNCH BEGINS	LUNCH ENDS	BREAK 2 BEGINS	BREAK 2 ENDS	CLOCK OUT	DAILY HOURS
	SUNDAY									
	MONDAY									
	TUESDAY									
	WEDNESDAY									
	THURSDAY									
	FRIDAY									
	SATURDAY									

TOTAL HOURS

REGULAR

OVERTIME

PAY RATE

REGULAR

OVERTIME

TOTAL PAY

REGULAR

OVERTIME

DATE OF PAYMENT

GROSS PAY $

TIME SHEET

EMPLOYEE

ID NUMBER

NAME

ADDRESS

DEPARTMENT

SUPERVISOR

COMPANY

NAME

ADDRESS

PHONE

PAY PERIOD BEGINNING

WEEK ONE

DATE	DAY OF THE WEEK	CLOCK IN	BREAK 1 BEGINS	BREAK 1 ENDS	LUNCH BEGINS	LUNCH ENDS	BREAK 2 BEGINS	BREAK 2 ENDS	CLOCK OUT	DAILY HOURS
	SUNDAY									
	MONDAY									
	TUESDAY									
	WEDNESDAY									
	THURSDAY									
	FRIDAY									
	SATURDAY									

WEEK TWO

DATE	DAY OF THE WEEK	CLOCK IN	BREAK 1 BEGINS	BREAK 1 ENDS	LUNCH BEGINS	LUNCH ENDS	BREAK 2 BEGINS	BREAK 2 ENDS	CLOCK OUT	DAILY HOURS
	SUNDAY									
	MONDAY									
	TUESDAY									
	WEDNESDAY									
	THURSDAY									
	FRIDAY									
	SATURDAY									

TOTAL HOURS		PAY RATE		TOTAL PAY	
REGULAR		REGULAR		REGULAR	
OVERTIME		OVERTIME		OVERTIME	

DATE OF PAYMENT		GROSS PAY	$

TIME SHEET

EMPLOYEE

ID NUMBER	
NAME	
ADDRESS	
DEPARTMENT	
SUPERVISOR	

COMPANY

NAME	
ADDRESS	
PHONE	
PAY PERIOD BEGINNING	

WEEK ONE

DATE	DAY OF THE WEEK	CLOCK IN	BREAK 1 BEGINS	BREAK 1 ENDS	LUNCH BEGINS	LUNCH ENDS	BREAK 2 BEGINS	BREAK 2 ENDS	CLOCK OUT	DAILY HOURS
	SUNDAY									
	MONDAY									
	TUESDAY									
	WEDNESDAY									
	THURSDAY									
	FRIDAY									
	SATURDAY									

WEEK TWO

DATE	DAY OF THE WEEK	CLOCK IN	BREAK 1 BEGINS	BREAK 1 ENDS	LUNCH BEGINS	LUNCH ENDS	BREAK 2 BEGINS	BREAK 2 ENDS	CLOCK OUT	DAILY HOURS
	SUNDAY									
	MONDAY									
	TUESDAY									
	WEDNESDAY									
	THURSDAY									
	FRIDAY									
	SATURDAY									

TOTAL HOURS		PAY RATE		TOTAL PAY	
REGULAR		REGULAR		REGULAR	
OVERTIME		OVERTIME		OVERTIME	

DATE OF PAYMENT			GROSS PAY	$

TIME SHEET

EMPLOYEE

ID NUMBER

NAME

ADDRESS

DEPARTMENT

SUPERVISOR

COMPANY

NAME

ADDRESS

PHONE

PAY PERIOD BEGINNING

WEEK ONE

DATE	DAY OF THE WEEK	CLOCK IN	BREAK 1 BEGINS	BREAK 1 ENDS	LUNCH BEGINS	LUNCH ENDS	BREAK 2 BEGINS	BREAK 2 ENDS	CLOCK OUT	DAILY HOURS
	SUNDAY									
	MONDAY									
	TUESDAY									
	WEDNESDAY									
	THURSDAY									
	FRIDAY									
	SATURDAY									

WEEK TWO

DATE	DAY OF THE WEEK	CLOCK IN	BREAK 1 BEGINS	BREAK 1 ENDS	LUNCH BEGINS	LUNCH ENDS	BREAK 2 BEGINS	BREAK 2 ENDS	CLOCK OUT	DAILY HOURS
	SUNDAY									
	MONDAY									
	TUESDAY									
	WEDNESDAY									
	THURSDAY									
	FRIDAY									
	SATURDAY									

TOTAL HOURS

REGULAR

OVERTIME

PAY RATE

REGULAR

OVERTIME

TOTAL PAY

REGULAR

OVERTIME

DATE OF PAYMENT

GROSS PAY $

TIME SHEET

EMPLOYEE

ID NUMBER

NAME

ADDRESS

DEPARTMENT

SUPERVISOR

COMPANY

NAME

ADDRESS

PHONE

PAY PERIOD BEGINNING

WEEK ONE

DATE	DAY OF THE WEEK	CLOCK IN	BREAK 1 BEGINS	BREAK 1 ENDS	LUNCH BEGINS	LUNCH ENDS	BREAK 2 BEGINS	BREAK 2 ENDS	CLOCK OUT	DAILY HOURS
	SUNDAY									
	MONDAY									
	TUESDAY									
	WEDNESDAY									
	THURSDAY									
	FRIDAY									
	SATURDAY									

WEEK TWO

DATE	DAY OF THE WEEK	CLOCK IN	BREAK 1 BEGINS	BREAK 1 ENDS	LUNCH BEGINS	LUNCH ENDS	BREAK 2 BEGINS	BREAK 2 ENDS	CLOCK OUT	DAILY HOURS
	SUNDAY									
	MONDAY									
	TUESDAY									
	WEDNESDAY									
	THURSDAY									
	FRIDAY									
	SATURDAY									

TOTAL HOURS		PAY RATE		TOTAL PAY	
REGULAR		REGULAR		REGULAR	
OVERTIME		OVERTIME		OVERTIME	
DATE OF PAYMENT				GROSS PAY	$

TIME SHEET

EMPLOYEE

ID NUMBER

NAME

ADDRESS

DEPARTMENT

SUPERVISOR

COMPANY

NAME

ADDRESS

PHONE

PAY PERIOD BEGINNING

WEEK ONE

DATE	DAY OF THE WEEK	CLOCK IN	BREAK 1 BEGINS	BREAK 1 ENDS	LUNCH BEGINS	LUNCH ENDS	BREAK 2 BEGINS	BREAK 2 ENDS	CLOCK OUT	DAILY HOURS
	SUNDAY									
	MONDAY									
	TUESDAY									
	WEDNESDAY									
	THURSDAY									
	FRIDAY									
	SATURDAY									

WEEK TWO

DATE	DAY OF THE WEEK	CLOCK IN	BREAK 1 BEGINS	BREAK 1 ENDS	LUNCH BEGINS	LUNCH ENDS	BREAK 2 BEGINS	BREAK 2 ENDS	CLOCK OUT	DAILY HOURS
	SUNDAY									
	MONDAY									
	TUESDAY									
	WEDNESDAY									
	THURSDAY									
	FRIDAY									
	SATURDAY									

TOTAL HOURS

REGULAR

OVERTIME

PAY RATE

REGULAR

OVERTIME

TOTAL PAY

REGULAR

OVERTIME

DATE OF PAYMENT

GROSS PAY $

TIME SHEET

<table>
<tr><th colspan="2">EMPLOYEE</th><th colspan="2">COMPANY</th></tr>
<tr><td>ID NUMBER</td><td></td><td>NAME</td><td></td></tr>
<tr><td>NAME</td><td></td><td rowspan="2">ADDRESS</td><td></td></tr>
<tr><td rowspan="2">ADDRESS</td><td></td><td></td></tr>
<tr><td></td><td></td><td></td></tr>
<tr><td>DEPARTMENT</td><td></td><td>PHONE</td><td></td></tr>
<tr><td>SUPERVISOR</td><td></td><td>PAY PERIOD BEGINNING</td><td></td></tr>
</table>

WEEK ONE

DATE	DAY OF THE WEEK	CLOCK IN	BREAK 1 BEGINS	BREAK 1 ENDS	LUNCH BEGINS	LUNCH ENDS	BREAK 2 BEGINS	BREAK 2 ENDS	CLOCK OUT	DAILY HOURS
	SUNDAY									
	MONDAY									
	TUESDAY									
	WEDNESDAY									
	THURSDAY									
	FRIDAY									
	SATURDAY									

WEEK TWO

DATE	DAY OF THE WEEK	CLOCK IN	BREAK 1 BEGINS	BREAK 1 ENDS	LUNCH BEGINS	LUNCH ENDS	BREAK 2 BEGINS	BREAK 2 ENDS	CLOCK OUT	DAILY HOURS
	SUNDAY									
	MONDAY									
	TUESDAY									
	WEDNESDAY									
	THURSDAY									
	FRIDAY									
	SATURDAY									

TOTAL HOURS		PAY RATE		TOTAL PAY	
REGULAR		REGULAR		REGULAR	
OVERTIME		OVERTIME		OVERTIME	
DATE OF PAYMENT				GROSS PAY	$

TIME SHEET

EMPLOYEE

ID NUMBER

NAME

ADDRESS

DEPARTMENT

SUPERVISOR

COMPANY

NAME

ADDRESS

PHONE

PAY PERIOD BEGINNING

WEEK ONE

DATE	DAY OF THE WEEK	CLOCK IN	BREAK 1 BEGINS	BREAK 1 ENDS	LUNCH BEGINS	LUNCH ENDS	BREAK 2 BEGINS	BREAK 2 ENDS	CLOCK OUT	DAILY HOURS
	SUNDAY									
	MONDAY									
	TUESDAY									
	WEDNESDAY									
	THURSDAY									
	FRIDAY									
	SATURDAY									

WEEK TWO

DATE	DAY OF THE WEEK	CLOCK IN	BREAK 1 BEGINS	BREAK 1 ENDS	LUNCH BEGINS	LUNCH ENDS	BREAK 2 BEGINS	BREAK 2 ENDS	CLOCK OUT	DAILY HOURS
	SUNDAY									
	MONDAY									
	TUESDAY									
	WEDNESDAY									
	THURSDAY									
	FRIDAY									
	SATURDAY									

TOTAL HOURS

REGULAR

OVERTIME

PAY RATE

REGULAR

OVERTIME

TOTAL PAY

REGULAR

OVERTIME

DATE OF PAYMENT

GROSS PAY $

TIME SHEET

EMPLOYEE

ID NUMBER

NAME

ADDRESS

DEPARTMENT

SUPERVISOR

COMPANY

NAME

ADDRESS

PHONE

PAY PERIOD BEGINNING

WEEK ONE

DATE	DAY OF THE WEEK	CLOCK IN	BREAK 1 BEGINS	BREAK 1 ENDS	LUNCH BEGINS	LUNCH ENDS	BREAK 2 BEGINS	BREAK 2 ENDS	CLOCK OUT	DAILY HOURS
	SUNDAY									
	MONDAY									
	TUESDAY									
	WEDNESDAY									
	THURSDAY									
	FRIDAY									
	SATURDAY									

WEEK TWO

DATE	DAY OF THE WEEK	CLOCK IN	BREAK 1 BEGINS	BREAK 1 ENDS	LUNCH BEGINS	LUNCH ENDS	BREAK 2 BEGINS	BREAK 2 ENDS	CLOCK OUT	DAILY HOURS
	SUNDAY									
	MONDAY									
	TUESDAY									
	WEDNESDAY									
	THURSDAY									
	FRIDAY									
	SATURDAY									

TOTAL HOURS

REGULAR

OVERTIME

PAY RATE

REGULAR

OVERTIME

TOTAL PAY

REGULAR

OVERTIME

DATE OF PAYMENT

GROSS PAY $

TIME SHEET

EMPLOYEE

ID NUMBER	
NAME	
ADDRESS	
DEPARTMENT	
SUPERVISOR	

COMPANY

NAME	
ADDRESS	
PHONE	
PAY PERIOD BEGINNING	

WEEK ONE

DATE	DAY OF THE WEEK	CLOCK IN	BREAK 1 BEGINS	BREAK 1 ENDS	LUNCH BEGINS	LUNCH ENDS	BREAK 2 BEGINS	BREAK 2 ENDS	CLOCK OUT	DAILY HOURS
	SUNDAY									
	MONDAY									
	TUESDAY									
	WEDNESDAY									
	THURSDAY									
	FRIDAY									
	SATURDAY									

WEEK TWO

DATE	DAY OF THE WEEK	CLOCK IN	BREAK 1 BEGINS	BREAK 1 ENDS	LUNCH BEGINS	LUNCH ENDS	BREAK 2 BEGINS	BREAK 2 ENDS	CLOCK OUT	DAILY HOURS
	SUNDAY									
	MONDAY									
	TUESDAY									
	WEDNESDAY									
	THURSDAY									
	FRIDAY									
	SATURDAY									

TOTAL HOURS | PAY RATE | TOTAL PAY

TOTAL HOURS		PAY RATE		TOTAL PAY	
REGULAR		REGULAR		REGULAR	
OVERTIME		OVERTIME		OVERTIME	

DATE OF PAYMENT		GROSS PAY	$

TIME SHEET

EMPLOYEE

ID NUMBER	
NAME	
ADDRESS	
DEPARTMENT	
SUPERVISOR	

COMPANY

NAME	
ADDRESS	
PHONE	
PAY PERIOD BEGINNING	

WEEK ONE

DATE	DAY OF THE WEEK	CLOCK IN	BREAK 1 BEGINS	BREAK 1 ENDS	LUNCH BEGINS	LUNCH ENDS	BREAK 2 BEGINS	BREAK 2 ENDS	CLOCK OUT	DAILY HOURS
	SUNDAY									
	MONDAY									
	TUESDAY									
	WEDNESDAY									
	THURSDAY									
	FRIDAY									
	SATURDAY									

WEEK TWO

DATE	DAY OF THE WEEK	CLOCK IN	BREAK 1 BEGINS	BREAK 1 ENDS	LUNCH BEGINS	LUNCH ENDS	BREAK 2 BEGINS	BREAK 2 ENDS	CLOCK OUT	DAILY HOURS
	SUNDAY									
	MONDAY									
	TUESDAY									
	WEDNESDAY									
	THURSDAY									
	FRIDAY									
	SATURDAY									

TOTAL HOURS | PAY RATE | TOTAL PAY

TOTAL HOURS		PAY RATE		TOTAL PAY	
REGULAR		REGULAR		REGULAR	
OVERTIME		OVERTIME		OVERTIME	

DATE OF PAYMENT		GROSS PAY	$

TIME SHEET

EMPLOYEE

ID NUMBER

NAME

ADDRESS

DEPARTMENT

SUPERVISOR

COMPANY

NAME

ADDRESS

PHONE

PAY PERIOD BEGINNING

WEEK ONE

DATE	DAY OF THE WEEK	CLOCK IN	BREAK 1 BEGINS	BREAK 1 ENDS	LUNCH BEGINS	LUNCH ENDS	BREAK 2 BEGINS	BREAK 2 ENDS	CLOCK OUT	DAILY HOURS
	SUNDAY									
	MONDAY									
	TUESDAY									
	WEDNESDAY									
	THURSDAY									
	FRIDAY									
	SATURDAY									

WEEK TWO

DATE	DAY OF THE WEEK	CLOCK IN	BREAK 1 BEGINS	BREAK 1 ENDS	LUNCH BEGINS	LUNCH ENDS	BREAK 2 BEGINS	BREAK 2 ENDS	CLOCK OUT	DAILY HOURS
	SUNDAY									
	MONDAY									
	TUESDAY									
	WEDNESDAY									
	THURSDAY									
	FRIDAY									
	SATURDAY									

TOTAL HOURS

REGULAR

OVERTIME

PAY RATE

REGULAR

OVERTIME

TOTAL PAY

REGULAR

OVERTIME

DATE OF PAYMENT

GROSS PAY $

TIME SHEET

EMPLOYEE

ID NUMBER	
NAME	
ADDRESS	
DEPARTMENT	
SUPERVISOR	

COMPANY

NAME	
ADDRESS	
PHONE	
PAY PERIOD BEGINNING	

WEEK ONE

DATE	DAY OF THE WEEK	CLOCK IN	BREAK 1 BEGINS	BREAK 1 ENDS	LUNCH BEGINS	LUNCH ENDS	BREAK 2 BEGINS	BREAK 2 ENDS	CLOCK OUT	DAILY HOURS
	SUNDAY									
	MONDAY									
	TUESDAY									
	WEDNESDAY									
	THURSDAY									
	FRIDAY									
	SATURDAY									

WEEK TWO

DATE	DAY OF THE WEEK	CLOCK IN	BREAK 1 BEGINS	BREAK 1 ENDS	LUNCH BEGINS	LUNCH ENDS	BREAK 2 BEGINS	BREAK 2 ENDS	CLOCK OUT	DAILY HOURS
	SUNDAY									
	MONDAY									
	TUESDAY									
	WEDNESDAY									
	THURSDAY									
	FRIDAY									
	SATURDAY									

TOTAL HOURS | PAY RATE | TOTAL PAY

TOTAL HOURS		PAY RATE		TOTAL PAY	
REGULAR		REGULAR		REGULAR	
OVERTIME		OVERTIME		OVERTIME	

DATE OF PAYMENT			GROSS PAY	$

TIME SHEET

EMPLOYEE

ID NUMBER

NAME

ADDRESS

DEPARTMENT

SUPERVISOR

COMPANY

NAME

ADDRESS

PHONE

PAY PERIOD BEGINNING

WEEK ONE

DATE	DAY OF THE WEEK	CLOCK IN	BREAK 1 BEGINS	BREAK 1 ENDS	LUNCH BEGINS	LUNCH ENDS	BREAK 2 BEGINS	BREAK 2 ENDS	CLOCK OUT	DAILY HOURS
	SUNDAY									
	MONDAY									
	TUESDAY									
	WEDNESDAY									
	THURSDAY									
	FRIDAY									
	SATURDAY									

WEEK TWO

DATE	DAY OF THE WEEK	CLOCK IN	BREAK 1 BEGINS	BREAK 1 ENDS	LUNCH BEGINS	LUNCH ENDS	BREAK 2 BEGINS	BREAK 2 ENDS	CLOCK OUT	DAILY HOURS
	SUNDAY									
	MONDAY									
	TUESDAY									
	WEDNESDAY									
	THURSDAY									
	FRIDAY									
	SATURDAY									

TOTAL HOURS

REGULAR

OVERTIME

PAY RATE

REGULAR

OVERTIME

TOTAL PAY

REGULAR

OVERTIME

DATE OF PAYMENT

GROSS PAY $

TIME SHEET

EMPLOYEE		COMPANY	
ID NUMBER		NAME	
NAME			
ADDRESS		ADDRESS	
DEPARTMENT		PHONE	
SUPERVISOR		PAY PERIOD BEGINNING	

WEEK ONE

DATE	DAY OF THE WEEK	CLOCK IN	BREAK 1 BEGINS	BREAK 1 ENDS	LUNCH BEGINS	LUNCH ENDS	BREAK 2 BEGINS	BREAK 2 ENDS	CLOCK OUT	DAILY HOURS
	SUNDAY									
	MONDAY									
	TUESDAY									
	WEDNESDAY									
	THURSDAY									
	FRIDAY									
	SATURDAY									

WEEK TWO

DATE	DAY OF THE WEEK	CLOCK IN	BREAK 1 BEGINS	BREAK 1 ENDS	LUNCH BEGINS	LUNCH ENDS	BREAK 2 BEGINS	BREAK 2 ENDS	CLOCK OUT	DAILY HOURS
	SUNDAY									
	MONDAY									
	TUESDAY									
	WEDNESDAY									
	THURSDAY									
	FRIDAY									
	SATURDAY									

TOTAL HOURS		PAY RATE		TOTAL PAY	
REGULAR		REGULAR		REGULAR	
OVERTIME		OVERTIME		OVERTIME	
DATE OF PAYMENT				GROSS PAY	$

TIME SHEET

EMPLOYEE

ID NUMBER

NAME

ADDRESS

DEPARTMENT

SUPERVISOR

COMPANY

NAME

ADDRESS

PHONE

PAY PERIOD BEGINNING

WEEK ONE

DATE	DAY OF THE WEEK	CLOCK IN	BREAK 1 BEGINS	BREAK 1 ENDS	LUNCH BEGINS	LUNCH ENDS	BREAK 2 BEGINS	BREAK 2 ENDS	CLOCK OUT	DAILY HOURS
	SUNDAY									
	MONDAY									
	TUESDAY									
	WEDNESDAY									
	THURSDAY									
	FRIDAY									
	SATURDAY									

WEEK TWO

DATE	DAY OF THE WEEK	CLOCK IN	BREAK 1 BEGINS	BREAK 1 ENDS	LUNCH BEGINS	LUNCH ENDS	BREAK 2 BEGINS	BREAK 2 ENDS	CLOCK OUT	DAILY HOURS
	SUNDAY									
	MONDAY									
	TUESDAY									
	WEDNESDAY									
	THURSDAY									
	FRIDAY									
	SATURDAY									

TOTAL HOURS / PAY RATE / TOTAL PAY

TOTAL HOURS		PAY RATE		TOTAL PAY	
REGULAR		REGULAR		REGULAR	
OVERTIME		OVERTIME		OVERTIME	

DATE OF PAYMENT

GROSS PAY $

TIME SHEET

EMPLOYEE

ID NUMBER

NAME

ADDRESS

DEPARTMENT

SUPERVISOR

COMPANY

NAME

ADDRESS

PHONE

PAY PERIOD BEGINNING

WEEK ONE

DATE	DAY OF THE WEEK	CLOCK IN	BREAK 1 BEGINS	BREAK 1 ENDS	LUNCH BEGINS	LUNCH ENDS	BREAK 2 BEGINS	BREAK 2 ENDS	CLOCK OUT	DAILY HOURS
	SUNDAY									
	MONDAY									
	TUESDAY									
	WEDNESDAY									
	THURSDAY									
	FRIDAY									
	SATURDAY									

WEEK TWO

DATE	DAY OF THE WEEK	CLOCK IN	BREAK 1 BEGINS	BREAK 1 ENDS	LUNCH BEGINS	LUNCH ENDS	BREAK 2 BEGINS	BREAK 2 ENDS	CLOCK OUT	DAILY HOURS
	SUNDAY									
	MONDAY									
	TUESDAY									
	WEDNESDAY									
	THURSDAY									
	FRIDAY									
	SATURDAY									

TOTAL HOURS		PAY RATE		TOTAL PAY	
REGULAR		REGULAR		REGULAR	
OVERTIME		OVERTIME		OVERTIME	
DATE OF PAYMENT				GROSS PAY	$

TIME SHEET

EMPLOYEE

ID NUMBER

NAME

ADDRESS

DEPARTMENT

SUPERVISOR

COMPANY

NAME

ADDRESS

PHONE

PAY PERIOD BEGINNING

WEEK ONE

DATE	DAY OF THE WEEK	CLOCK IN	BREAK 1 BEGINS	BREAK 1 ENDS	LUNCH BEGINS	LUNCH ENDS	BREAK 2 BEGINS	BREAK 2 ENDS	CLOCK OUT	DAILY HOURS
	SUNDAY									
	MONDAY									
	TUESDAY									
	WEDNESDAY									
	THURSDAY									
	FRIDAY									
	SATURDAY									

WEEK TWO

DATE	DAY OF THE WEEK	CLOCK IN	BREAK 1 BEGINS	BREAK 1 ENDS	LUNCH BEGINS	LUNCH ENDS	BREAK 2 BEGINS	BREAK 2 ENDS	CLOCK OUT	DAILY HOURS
	SUNDAY									
	MONDAY									
	TUESDAY									
	WEDNESDAY									
	THURSDAY									
	FRIDAY									
	SATURDAY									

TOTAL HOURS		PAY RATE		TOTAL PAY	
REGULAR		REGULAR		REGULAR	
OVERTIME		OVERTIME		OVERTIME	
DATE OF PAYMENT				GROSS PAY	$

TIME SHEET

EMPLOYEE

ID NUMBER	
NAME	
ADDRESS	
DEPARTMENT	
SUPERVISOR	

COMPANY

NAME	
ADDRESS	
PHONE	
PAY PERIOD BEGINNING	

WEEK ONE

DATE	DAY OF THE WEEK	CLOCK IN	BREAK 1 BEGINS	BREAK 1 ENDS	LUNCH BEGINS	LUNCH ENDS	BREAK 2 BEGINS	BREAK 2 ENDS	CLOCK OUT	DAILY HOURS
	SUNDAY									
	MONDAY									
	TUESDAY									
	WEDNESDAY									
	THURSDAY									
	FRIDAY									
	SATURDAY									

WEEK TWO

DATE	DAY OF THE WEEK	CLOCK IN	BREAK 1 BEGINS	BREAK 1 ENDS	LUNCH BEGINS	LUNCH ENDS	BREAK 2 BEGINS	BREAK 2 ENDS	CLOCK OUT	DAILY HOURS
	SUNDAY									
	MONDAY									
	TUESDAY									
	WEDNESDAY									
	THURSDAY									
	FRIDAY									
	SATURDAY									

TOTAL HOURS / PAY RATE / TOTAL PAY

TOTAL HOURS		PAY RATE		TOTAL PAY	
REGULAR		REGULAR		REGULAR	
OVERTIME		OVERTIME		OVERTIME	

DATE OF PAYMENT			GROSS PAY	$

TIME SHEET

EMPLOYEE

ID NUMBER	
NAME	
ADDRESS	
DEPARTMENT	
SUPERVISOR	

COMPANY

NAME	
ADDRESS	
PHONE	
PAY PERIOD BEGINNING	

WEEK ONE

DATE	DAY OF THE WEEK	CLOCK IN	BREAK 1 BEGINS	BREAK 1 ENDS	LUNCH BEGINS	LUNCH ENDS	BREAK 2 BEGINS	BREAK 2 ENDS	CLOCK OUT	DAILY HOURS
	SUNDAY									
	MONDAY									
	TUESDAY									
	WEDNESDAY									
	THURSDAY									
	FRIDAY									
	SATURDAY									

WEEK TWO

DATE	DAY OF THE WEEK	CLOCK IN	BREAK 1 BEGINS	BREAK 1 ENDS	LUNCH BEGINS	LUNCH ENDS	BREAK 2 BEGINS	BREAK 2 ENDS	CLOCK OUT	DAILY HOURS
	SUNDAY									
	MONDAY									
	TUESDAY									
	WEDNESDAY									
	THURSDAY									
	FRIDAY									
	SATURDAY									

TOTAL HOURS

REGULAR	
OVERTIME	

PAY RATE

REGULAR	
OVERTIME	

TOTAL PAY

REGULAR	
OVERTIME	

DATE OF PAYMENT		GROSS PAY	$

TIME SHEET

EMPLOYEE

ID NUMBER

NAME

ADDRESS

DEPARTMENT

SUPERVISOR

COMPANY

NAME

ADDRESS

PHONE

PAY PERIOD BEGINNING

WEEK ONE

DATE	DAY OF THE WEEK	CLOCK IN	BREAK 1 BEGINS	BREAK 1 ENDS	LUNCH BEGINS	LUNCH ENDS	BREAK 2 BEGINS	BREAK 2 ENDS	CLOCK OUT	DAILY HOURS
	SUNDAY									
	MONDAY									
	TUESDAY									
	WEDNESDAY									
	THURSDAY									
	FRIDAY									
	SATURDAY									

WEEK TWO

DATE	DAY OF THE WEEK	CLOCK IN	BREAK 1 BEGINS	BREAK 1 ENDS	LUNCH BEGINS	LUNCH ENDS	BREAK 2 BEGINS	BREAK 2 ENDS	CLOCK OUT	DAILY HOURS
	SUNDAY									
	MONDAY									
	TUESDAY									
	WEDNESDAY									
	THURSDAY									
	FRIDAY									
	SATURDAY									

TOTAL HOURS		PAY RATE		TOTAL PAY	
REGULAR		REGULAR		REGULAR	
OVERTIME		OVERTIME		OVERTIME	
DATE OF PAYMENT				GROSS PAY	$

TIME SHEET

EMPLOYEE

ID NUMBER

NAME

ADDRESS

DEPARTMENT

SUPERVISOR

COMPANY

NAME

ADDRESS

PHONE

PAY PERIOD BEGINNING

WEEK ONE

DATE	DAY OF THE WEEK	CLOCK IN	BREAK 1 BEGINS	BREAK 1 ENDS	LUNCH BEGINS	LUNCH ENDS	BREAK 2 BEGINS	BREAK 2 ENDS	CLOCK OUT	DAILY HOURS
	SUNDAY									
	MONDAY									
	TUESDAY									
	WEDNESDAY									
	THURSDAY									
	FRIDAY									
	SATURDAY									

WEEK TWO

DATE	DAY OF THE WEEK	CLOCK IN	BREAK 1 BEGINS	BREAK 1 ENDS	LUNCH BEGINS	LUNCH ENDS	BREAK 2 BEGINS	BREAK 2 ENDS	CLOCK OUT	DAILY HOURS
	SUNDAY									
	MONDAY									
	TUESDAY									
	WEDNESDAY									
	THURSDAY									
	FRIDAY									
	SATURDAY									

TOTAL HOURS

REGULAR

OVERTIME

PAY RATE

REGULAR

OVERTIME

TOTAL PAY

REGULAR

OVERTIME

| DATE OF PAYMENT | | GROSS PAY | $ |

TIME SHEET

EMPLOYEE

ID NUMBER	
NAME	
ADDRESS	
DEPARTMENT	
SUPERVISOR	

COMPANY

NAME	
ADDRESS	
PHONE	
PAY PERIOD BEGINNING	

WEEK ONE

DATE	DAY OF THE WEEK	CLOCK IN	BREAK 1 BEGINS	BREAK 1 ENDS	LUNCH BEGINS	LUNCH ENDS	BREAK 2 BEGINS	BREAK 2 ENDS	CLOCK OUT	DAILY HOURS
	SUNDAY									
	MONDAY									
	TUESDAY									
	WEDNESDAY									
	THURSDAY									
	FRIDAY									
	SATURDAY									

WEEK TWO

DATE	DAY OF THE WEEK	CLOCK IN	BREAK 1 BEGINS	BREAK 1 ENDS	LUNCH BEGINS	LUNCH ENDS	BREAK 2 BEGINS	BREAK 2 ENDS	CLOCK OUT	DAILY HOURS
	SUNDAY									
	MONDAY									
	TUESDAY									
	WEDNESDAY									
	THURSDAY									
	FRIDAY									
	SATURDAY									

TOTAL HOURS / PAY RATE / TOTAL PAY

TOTAL HOURS		PAY RATE		TOTAL PAY	
REGULAR		REGULAR		REGULAR	
OVERTIME		OVERTIME		OVERTIME	

DATE OF PAYMENT		GROSS PAY	$

TIME SHEET

EMPLOYEE

ID NUMBER

NAME

ADDRESS

DEPARTMENT

SUPERVISOR

COMPANY

NAME

ADDRESS

PHONE

PAY PERIOD BEGINNING

WEEK ONE

DATE	DAY OF THE WEEK	CLOCK IN	BREAK 1 BEGINS	BREAK 1 ENDS	LUNCH BEGINS	LUNCH ENDS	BREAK 2 BEGINS	BREAK 2 ENDS	CLOCK OUT	DAILY HOURS
	SUNDAY									
	MONDAY									
	TUESDAY									
	WEDNESDAY									
	THURSDAY									
	FRIDAY									
	SATURDAY									

WEEK TWO

DATE	DAY OF THE WEEK	CLOCK IN	BREAK 1 BEGINS	BREAK 1 ENDS	LUNCH BEGINS	LUNCH ENDS	BREAK 2 BEGINS	BREAK 2 ENDS	CLOCK OUT	DAILY HOURS
	SUNDAY									
	MONDAY									
	TUESDAY									
	WEDNESDAY									
	THURSDAY									
	FRIDAY									
	SATURDAY									

TOTAL HOURS

REGULAR

OVERTIME

PAY RATE

REGULAR

OVERTIME

TOTAL PAY

REGULAR

OVERTIME

DATE OF PAYMENT

GROSS PAY $

TIME SHEET

EMPLOYEE

ID NUMBER

NAME

ADDRESS

DEPARTMENT

SUPERVISOR

COMPANY

NAME

ADDRESS

PHONE

PAY PERIOD BEGINNING

WEEK ONE

DATE	DAY OF THE WEEK	CLOCK IN	BREAK 1 BEGINS	BREAK 1 ENDS	LUNCH BEGINS	LUNCH ENDS	BREAK 2 BEGINS	BREAK 2 ENDS	CLOCK OUT	DAILY HOURS
	SUNDAY									
	MONDAY									
	TUESDAY									
	WEDNESDAY									
	THURSDAY									
	FRIDAY									
	SATURDAY									

WEEK TWO

DATE	DAY OF THE WEEK	CLOCK IN	BREAK 1 BEGINS	BREAK 1 ENDS	LUNCH BEGINS	LUNCH ENDS	BREAK 2 BEGINS	BREAK 2 ENDS	CLOCK OUT	DAILY HOURS
	SUNDAY									
	MONDAY									
	TUESDAY									
	WEDNESDAY									
	THURSDAY									
	FRIDAY									
	SATURDAY									

TOTAL HOURS

REGULAR

OVERTIME

PAY RATE

REGULAR

OVERTIME

TOTAL PAY

REGULAR

OVERTIME

DATE OF PAYMENT

GROSS PAY $

TIME SHEET

EMPLOYEE

ID NUMBER

NAME

ADDRESS

DEPARTMENT

SUPERVISOR

COMPANY

NAME

ADDRESS

PHONE

PAY PERIOD BEGINNING

WEEK ONE

DATE	DAY OF THE WEEK	CLOCK IN	BREAK 1 BEGINS	BREAK 1 ENDS	LUNCH BEGINS	LUNCH ENDS	BREAK 2 BEGINS	BREAK 2 ENDS	CLOCK OUT	DAILY HOURS
	SUNDAY									
	MONDAY									
	TUESDAY									
	WEDNESDAY									
	THURSDAY									
	FRIDAY									
	SATURDAY									

WEEK TWO

DATE	DAY OF THE WEEK	CLOCK IN	BREAK 1 BEGINS	BREAK 1 ENDS	LUNCH BEGINS	LUNCH ENDS	BREAK 2 BEGINS	BREAK 2 ENDS	CLOCK OUT	DAILY HOURS
	SUNDAY									
	MONDAY									
	TUESDAY									
	WEDNESDAY									
	THURSDAY									
	FRIDAY									
	SATURDAY									

TOTAL HOURS

REGULAR

OVERTIME

PAY RATE

REGULAR

OVERTIME

TOTAL PAY

REGULAR

OVERTIME

DATE OF PAYMENT

GROSS PAY $

TIME SHEET

EMPLOYEE

ID NUMBER

NAME

ADDRESS

DEPARTMENT

SUPERVISOR

COMPANY

NAME

ADDRESS

PHONE

PAY PERIOD BEGINNING

WEEK ONE

DATE	DAY OF THE WEEK	CLOCK IN	BREAK 1 BEGINS	BREAK 1 ENDS	LUNCH BEGINS	LUNCH ENDS	BREAK 2 BEGINS	BREAK 2 ENDS	CLOCK OUT	DAILY HOURS
	SUNDAY									
	MONDAY									
	TUESDAY									
	WEDNESDAY									
	THURSDAY									
	FRIDAY									
	SATURDAY									

WEEK TWO

DATE	DAY OF THE WEEK	CLOCK IN	BREAK 1 BEGINS	BREAK 1 ENDS	LUNCH BEGINS	LUNCH ENDS	BREAK 2 BEGINS	BREAK 2 ENDS	CLOCK OUT	DAILY HOURS
	SUNDAY									
	MONDAY									
	TUESDAY									
	WEDNESDAY									
	THURSDAY									
	FRIDAY									
	SATURDAY									

TOTAL HOURS | PAY RATE | TOTAL PAY

TOTAL HOURS		PAY RATE		TOTAL PAY	
REGULAR		REGULAR		REGULAR	
OVERTIME		OVERTIME		OVERTIME	

DATE OF PAYMENT		GROSS PAY	$

TIME SHEET

EMPLOYEE

ID NUMBER

NAME

ADDRESS

DEPARTMENT

SUPERVISOR

COMPANY

NAME

ADDRESS

PHONE

PAY PERIOD BEGINNING

WEEK ONE

DATE	DAY OF THE WEEK	CLOCK IN	BREAK 1 BEGINS	BREAK 1 ENDS	LUNCH BEGINS	LUNCH ENDS	BREAK 2 BEGINS	BREAK 2 ENDS	CLOCK OUT	DAILY HOURS
	SUNDAY									
	MONDAY									
	TUESDAY									
	WEDNESDAY									
	THURSDAY									
	FRIDAY									
	SATURDAY									

WEEK TWO

DATE	DAY OF THE WEEK	CLOCK IN	BREAK 1 BEGINS	BREAK 1 ENDS	LUNCH BEGINS	LUNCH ENDS	BREAK 2 BEGINS	BREAK 2 ENDS	CLOCK OUT	DAILY HOURS
	SUNDAY									
	MONDAY									
	TUESDAY									
	WEDNESDAY									
	THURSDAY									
	FRIDAY									
	SATURDAY									

TOTAL HOURS

REGULAR

OVERTIME

PAY RATE

REGULAR

OVERTIME

TOTAL PAY

REGULAR

OVERTIME

DATE OF PAYMENT

GROSS PAY $

TIME SHEET

EMPLOYEE

ID NUMBER

NAME

ADDRESS

DEPARTMENT

SUPERVISOR

COMPANY

NAME

ADDRESS

PHONE

PAY PERIOD BEGINNING

WEEK ONE

DATE	DAY OF THE WEEK	CLOCK IN	BREAK 1 BEGINS	BREAK 1 ENDS	LUNCH BEGINS	LUNCH ENDS	BREAK 2 BEGINS	BREAK 2 ENDS	CLOCK OUT	DAILY HOURS
	SUNDAY									
	MONDAY									
	TUESDAY									
	WEDNESDAY									
	THURSDAY									
	FRIDAY									
	SATURDAY									

WEEK TWO

DATE	DAY OF THE WEEK	CLOCK IN	BREAK 1 BEGINS	BREAK 1 ENDS	LUNCH BEGINS	LUNCH ENDS	BREAK 2 BEGINS	BREAK 2 ENDS	CLOCK OUT	DAILY HOURS
	SUNDAY									
	MONDAY									
	TUESDAY									
	WEDNESDAY									
	THURSDAY									
	FRIDAY									
	SATURDAY									

TOTAL HOURS

REGULAR

OVERTIME

PAY RATE

REGULAR

OVERTIME

TOTAL PAY

REGULAR

OVERTIME

DATE OF PAYMENT

GROSS PAY $

TIME SHEET

EMPLOYEE

ID NUMBER

NAME

ADDRESS

DEPARTMENT

SUPERVISOR

COMPANY

NAME

ADDRESS

PHONE

PAY PERIOD BEGINNING

WEEK ONE

DATE	DAY OF THE WEEK	CLOCK IN	BREAK 1 BEGINS	BREAK 1 ENDS	LUNCH BEGINS	LUNCH ENDS	BREAK 2 BEGINS	BREAK 2 ENDS	CLOCK OUT	DAILY HOURS
	SUNDAY									
	MONDAY									
	TUESDAY									
	WEDNESDAY									
	THURSDAY									
	FRIDAY									
	SATURDAY									

WEEK TWO

DATE	DAY OF THE WEEK	CLOCK IN	BREAK 1 BEGINS	BREAK 1 ENDS	LUNCH BEGINS	LUNCH ENDS	BREAK 2 BEGINS	BREAK 2 ENDS	CLOCK OUT	DAILY HOURS
	SUNDAY									
	MONDAY									
	TUESDAY									
	WEDNESDAY									
	THURSDAY									
	FRIDAY									
	SATURDAY									

TOTAL HOURS		PAY RATE		TOTAL PAY	
REGULAR		REGULAR		REGULAR	
OVERTIME		OVERTIME		OVERTIME	

DATE OF PAYMENT		GROSS PAY	$

TIME SHEET

<table>
<tr><th colspan="2">EMPLOYEE</th><th colspan="2">COMPANY</th></tr>
<tr><td>ID NUMBER</td><td></td><td>NAME</td><td></td></tr>
<tr><td>NAME</td><td></td><td></td><td></td></tr>
<tr><td>ADDRESS</td><td></td><td>ADDRESS</td><td></td></tr>
<tr><td></td><td></td><td></td><td></td></tr>
<tr><td>DEPARTMENT</td><td></td><td>PHONE</td><td></td></tr>
<tr><td>SUPERVISOR</td><td></td><td>PAY PERIOD BEGINNING</td><td></td></tr>
</table>

WEEK ONE

DATE	DAY OF THE WEEK	CLOCK IN	BREAK 1 BEGINS	BREAK 1 ENDS	LUNCH BEGINS	LUNCH ENDS	BREAK 2 BEGINS	BREAK 2 ENDS	CLOCK OUT	DAILY HOURS
	SUNDAY									
	MONDAY									
	TUESDAY									
	WEDNESDAY									
	THURSDAY									
	FRIDAY									
	SATURDAY									

WEEK TWO

DATE	DAY OF THE WEEK	CLOCK IN	BREAK 1 BEGINS	BREAK 1 ENDS	LUNCH BEGINS	LUNCH ENDS	BREAK 2 BEGINS	BREAK 2 ENDS	CLOCK OUT	DAILY HOURS
	SUNDAY									
	MONDAY									
	TUESDAY									
	WEDNESDAY									
	THURSDAY									
	FRIDAY									
	SATURDAY									

TOTAL HOURS		PAY RATE		TOTAL PAY	
REGULAR		REGULAR		REGULAR	
OVERTIME		OVERTIME		OVERTIME	
DATE OF PAYMENT				GROSS PAY	$

TIME SHEET

EMPLOYEE

ID NUMBER

NAME

ADDRESS

DEPARTMENT

SUPERVISOR

COMPANY

NAME

ADDRESS

PHONE

PAY PERIOD BEGINNING

WEEK ONE

DATE	DAY OF THE WEEK	CLOCK IN	BREAK 1 BEGINS	BREAK 1 ENDS	LUNCH BEGINS	LUNCH ENDS	BREAK 2 BEGINS	BREAK 2 ENDS	CLOCK OUT	DAILY HOURS
	SUNDAY									
	MONDAY									
	TUESDAY									
	WEDNESDAY									
	THURSDAY									
	FRIDAY									
	SATURDAY									

WEEK TWO

DATE	DAY OF THE WEEK	CLOCK IN	BREAK 1 BEGINS	BREAK 1 ENDS	LUNCH BEGINS	LUNCH ENDS	BREAK 2 BEGINS	BREAK 2 ENDS	CLOCK OUT	DAILY HOURS
	SUNDAY									
	MONDAY									
	TUESDAY									
	WEDNESDAY									
	THURSDAY									
	FRIDAY									
	SATURDAY									

TOTAL HOURS

REGULAR

OVERTIME

PAY RATE

REGULAR

OVERTIME

TOTAL PAY

REGULAR

OVERTIME

DATE OF PAYMENT

GROSS PAY $

TIME SHEET

<table>
<tr><th colspan="2">EMPLOYEE</th><th colspan="2">COMPANY</th></tr>
<tr><td>ID NUMBER</td><td></td><td>NAME</td><td></td></tr>
<tr><td>NAME</td><td></td><td rowspan="2">ADDRESS</td><td></td></tr>
<tr><td rowspan="2">ADDRESS</td><td></td><td></td></tr>
<tr><td></td><td></td><td></td></tr>
<tr><td>DEPARTMENT</td><td></td><td>PHONE</td><td></td></tr>
<tr><td>SUPERVISOR</td><td></td><td>PAY PERIOD BEGINNING</td><td></td></tr>
</table>

WEEK ONE

DATE	DAY OF THE WEEK	CLOCK IN	BREAK 1 BEGINS	BREAK 1 ENDS	LUNCH BEGINS	LUNCH ENDS	BREAK 2 BEGINS	BREAK 2 ENDS	CLOCK OUT	DAILY HOURS
	SUNDAY									
	MONDAY									
	TUESDAY									
	WEDNESDAY									
	THURSDAY									
	FRIDAY									
	SATURDAY									

WEEK TWO

DATE	DAY OF THE WEEK	CLOCK IN	BREAK 1 BEGINS	BREAK 1 ENDS	LUNCH BEGINS	LUNCH ENDS	BREAK 2 BEGINS	BREAK 2 ENDS	CLOCK OUT	DAILY HOURS
	SUNDAY									
	MONDAY									
	TUESDAY									
	WEDNESDAY									
	THURSDAY									
	FRIDAY									
	SATURDAY									

TOTAL HOURS		PAY RATE		TOTAL PAY	
REGULAR		REGULAR		REGULAR	
OVERTIME		OVERTIME		OVERTIME	
DATE OF PAYMENT				GROSS PAY	$

TIME SHEET

EMPLOYEE

ID NUMBER

NAME

ADDRESS

DEPARTMENT

SUPERVISOR

COMPANY

NAME

ADDRESS

PHONE

PAY PERIOD BEGINNING

WEEK ONE

DATE	DAY OF THE WEEK	CLOCK IN	BREAK 1 BEGINS	BREAK 1 ENDS	LUNCH BEGINS	LUNCH ENDS	BREAK 2 BEGINS	BREAK 2 ENDS	CLOCK OUT	DAILY HOURS
	SUNDAY									
	MONDAY									
	TUESDAY									
	WEDNESDAY									
	THURSDAY									
	FRIDAY									
	SATURDAY									

WEEK TWO

DATE	DAY OF THE WEEK	CLOCK IN	BREAK 1 BEGINS	BREAK 1 ENDS	LUNCH BEGINS	LUNCH ENDS	BREAK 2 BEGINS	BREAK 2 ENDS	CLOCK OUT	DAILY HOURS
	SUNDAY									
	MONDAY									
	TUESDAY									
	WEDNESDAY									
	THURSDAY									
	FRIDAY									
	SATURDAY									

TOTAL HOURS		PAY RATE		TOTAL PAY	
REGULAR		REGULAR		REGULAR	
OVERTIME		OVERTIME		OVERTIME	
DATE OF PAYMENT				GROSS PAY	$

TIME SHEET

EMPLOYEE

ID NUMBER

NAME

ADDRESS

DEPARTMENT

SUPERVISOR

COMPANY

NAME

ADDRESS

PHONE

PAY PERIOD BEGINNING

WEEK ONE

DATE	DAY OF THE WEEK	CLOCK IN	BREAK 1 BEGINS	BREAK 1 ENDS	LUNCH BEGINS	LUNCH ENDS	BREAK 2 BEGINS	BREAK 2 ENDS	CLOCK OUT	DAILY HOURS
	SUNDAY									
	MONDAY									
	TUESDAY									
	WEDNESDAY									
	THURSDAY									
	FRIDAY									
	SATURDAY									

WEEK TWO

DATE	DAY OF THE WEEK	CLOCK IN	BREAK 1 BEGINS	BREAK 1 ENDS	LUNCH BEGINS	LUNCH ENDS	BREAK 2 BEGINS	BREAK 2 ENDS	CLOCK OUT	DAILY HOURS
	SUNDAY									
	MONDAY									
	TUESDAY									
	WEDNESDAY									
	THURSDAY									
	FRIDAY									
	SATURDAY									

TOTAL HOURS		PAY RATE		TOTAL PAY	
REGULAR		REGULAR		REGULAR	
OVERTIME		OVERTIME		OVERTIME	
DATE OF PAYMENT				GROSS PAY	$

TIME SHEET

EMPLOYEE

ID NUMBER

NAME

ADDRESS

DEPARTMENT

SUPERVISOR

COMPANY

NAME

ADDRESS

PHONE

PAY PERIOD BEGINNING

WEEK ONE

DATE	DAY OF THE WEEK	CLOCK IN	BREAK 1 BEGINS	BREAK 1 ENDS	LUNCH BEGINS	LUNCH ENDS	BREAK 2 BEGINS	BREAK 2 ENDS	CLOCK OUT	DAILY HOURS
	SUNDAY									
	MONDAY									
	TUESDAY									
	WEDNESDAY									
	THURSDAY									
	FRIDAY									
	SATURDAY									

WEEK TWO

DATE	DAY OF THE WEEK	CLOCK IN	BREAK 1 BEGINS	BREAK 1 ENDS	LUNCH BEGINS	LUNCH ENDS	BREAK 2 BEGINS	BREAK 2 ENDS	CLOCK OUT	DAILY HOURS
	SUNDAY									
	MONDAY									
	TUESDAY									
	WEDNESDAY									
	THURSDAY									
	FRIDAY									
	SATURDAY									

TOTAL HOURS

REGULAR

OVERTIME

PAY RATE

REGULAR

OVERTIME

TOTAL PAY

REGULAR

OVERTIME

DATE OF PAYMENT

GROSS PAY $

TIME SHEET

EMPLOYEE

ID NUMBER

NAME

ADDRESS

DEPARTMENT

SUPERVISOR

COMPANY

NAME

ADDRESS

PHONE

PAY PERIOD BEGINNING

WEEK ONE

DATE	DAY OF THE WEEK	CLOCK IN	BREAK 1 BEGINS	BREAK 1 ENDS	LUNCH BEGINS	LUNCH ENDS	BREAK 2 BEGINS	BREAK 2 ENDS	CLOCK OUT	DAILY HOURS
	SUNDAY									
	MONDAY									
	TUESDAY									
	WEDNESDAY									
	THURSDAY									
	FRIDAY									
	SATURDAY									

WEEK TWO

DATE	DAY OF THE WEEK	CLOCK IN	BREAK 1 BEGINS	BREAK 1 ENDS	LUNCH BEGINS	LUNCH ENDS	BREAK 2 BEGINS	BREAK 2 ENDS	CLOCK OUT	DAILY HOURS
	SUNDAY									
	MONDAY									
	TUESDAY									
	WEDNESDAY									
	THURSDAY									
	FRIDAY									
	SATURDAY									

TOTAL HOURS | PAY RATE | TOTAL PAY

TOTAL HOURS		PAY RATE		TOTAL PAY	
REGULAR		REGULAR		REGULAR	
OVERTIME		OVERTIME		OVERTIME	

DATE OF PAYMENT		GROSS PAY	$

TIME SHEET

EMPLOYEE

ID NUMBER

NAME

ADDRESS

DEPARTMENT

SUPERVISOR

COMPANY

NAME

ADDRESS

PHONE

PAY PERIOD BEGINNING

WEEK ONE

DATE	DAY OF THE WEEK	CLOCK IN	BREAK 1 BEGINS	BREAK 1 ENDS	LUNCH BEGINS	LUNCH ENDS	BREAK 2 BEGINS	BREAK 2 ENDS	CLOCK OUT	DAILY HOURS
	SUNDAY									
	MONDAY									
	TUESDAY									
	WEDNESDAY									
	THURSDAY									
	FRIDAY									
	SATURDAY									

WEEK TWO

DATE	DAY OF THE WEEK	CLOCK IN	BREAK 1 BEGINS	BREAK 1 ENDS	LUNCH BEGINS	LUNCH ENDS	BREAK 2 BEGINS	BREAK 2 ENDS	CLOCK OUT	DAILY HOURS
	SUNDAY									
	MONDAY									
	TUESDAY									
	WEDNESDAY									
	THURSDAY									
	FRIDAY									
	SATURDAY									

TOTAL HOURS

REGULAR

OVERTIME

PAY RATE

REGULAR

OVERTIME

TOTAL PAY

REGULAR

OVERTIME

DATE OF PAYMENT

GROSS PAY $

TIME SHEET

EMPLOYEE

ID NUMBER

NAME

ADDRESS

DEPARTMENT

SUPERVISOR

COMPANY

NAME

ADDRESS

PHONE

PAY PERIOD BEGINNING

WEEK ONE

DATE	DAY OF THE WEEK	CLOCK IN	BREAK 1 BEGINS	BREAK 1 ENDS	LUNCH BEGINS	LUNCH ENDS	BREAK 2 BEGINS	BREAK 2 ENDS	CLOCK OUT	DAILY HOURS
	SUNDAY									
	MONDAY									
	TUESDAY									
	WEDNESDAY									
	THURSDAY									
	FRIDAY									
	SATURDAY									

WEEK TWO

DATE	DAY OF THE WEEK	CLOCK IN	BREAK 1 BEGINS	BREAK 1 ENDS	LUNCH BEGINS	LUNCH ENDS	BREAK 2 BEGINS	BREAK 2 ENDS	CLOCK OUT	DAILY HOURS
	SUNDAY									
	MONDAY									
	TUESDAY									
	WEDNESDAY									
	THURSDAY									
	FRIDAY									
	SATURDAY									

TOTAL HOURS		PAY RATE		TOTAL PAY	
REGULAR		REGULAR		REGULAR	
OVERTIME		OVERTIME		OVERTIME	
DATE OF PAYMENT				GROSS PAY	$

TIME SHEET

EMPLOYEE

ID NUMBER

NAME

ADDRESS

DEPARTMENT

SUPERVISOR

COMPANY

NAME

ADDRESS

PHONE

PAY PERIOD BEGINNING

WEEK ONE

DATE	DAY OF THE WEEK	CLOCK IN	BREAK 1 BEGINS	BREAK 1 ENDS	LUNCH BEGINS	LUNCH ENDS	BREAK 2 BEGINS	BREAK 2 ENDS	CLOCK OUT	DAILY HOURS
	SUNDAY									
	MONDAY									
	TUESDAY									
	WEDNESDAY									
	THURSDAY									
	FRIDAY									
	SATURDAY									

WEEK TWO

DATE	DAY OF THE WEEK	CLOCK IN	BREAK 1 BEGINS	BREAK 1 ENDS	LUNCH BEGINS	LUNCH ENDS	BREAK 2 BEGINS	BREAK 2 ENDS	CLOCK OUT	DAILY HOURS
	SUNDAY									
	MONDAY									
	TUESDAY									
	WEDNESDAY									
	THURSDAY									
	FRIDAY									
	SATURDAY									

TOTAL HOURS		PAY RATE		TOTAL PAY	
REGULAR		REGULAR		REGULAR	
OVERTIME		OVERTIME		OVERTIME	
DATE OF PAYMENT				GROSS PAY	$

TIME SHEET

EMPLOYEE

ID NUMBER	
NAME	
ADDRESS	
DEPARTMENT	
SUPERVISOR	

COMPANY

NAME	
ADDRESS	
PHONE	
PAY PERIOD BEGINNING	

WEEK ONE

DATE	DAY OF THE WEEK	CLOCK IN	BREAK 1 BEGINS	BREAK 1 ENDS	LUNCH BEGINS	LUNCH ENDS	BREAK 2 BEGINS	BREAK 2 ENDS	CLOCK OUT	DAILY HOURS
	SUNDAY									
	MONDAY									
	TUESDAY									
	WEDNESDAY									
	THURSDAY									
	FRIDAY									
	SATURDAY									

WEEK TWO

DATE	DAY OF THE WEEK	CLOCK IN	BREAK 1 BEGINS	BREAK 1 ENDS	LUNCH BEGINS	LUNCH ENDS	BREAK 2 BEGINS	BREAK 2 ENDS	CLOCK OUT	DAILY HOURS
	SUNDAY									
	MONDAY									
	TUESDAY									
	WEDNESDAY									
	THURSDAY									
	FRIDAY									
	SATURDAY									

TOTAL HOURS		PAY RATE		TOTAL PAY	
REGULAR		REGULAR		REGULAR	
OVERTIME		OVERTIME		OVERTIME	
DATE OF PAYMENT				GROSS PAY	$

TIME SHEET

EMPLOYEE

ID NUMBER

NAME

ADDRESS

DEPARTMENT

SUPERVISOR

COMPANY

NAME

ADDRESS

PHONE

PAY PERIOD BEGINNING

WEEK ONE

DATE	DAY OF THE WEEK	CLOCK IN	BREAK 1 BEGINS	BREAK 1 ENDS	LUNCH BEGINS	LUNCH ENDS	BREAK 2 BEGINS	BREAK 2 ENDS	CLOCK OUT	DAILY HOURS
	SUNDAY									
	MONDAY									
	TUESDAY									
	WEDNESDAY									
	THURSDAY									
	FRIDAY									
	SATURDAY									

WEEK TWO

DATE	DAY OF THE WEEK	CLOCK IN	BREAK 1 BEGINS	BREAK 1 ENDS	LUNCH BEGINS	LUNCH ENDS	BREAK 2 BEGINS	BREAK 2 ENDS	CLOCK OUT	DAILY HOURS
	SUNDAY									
	MONDAY									
	TUESDAY									
	WEDNESDAY									
	THURSDAY									
	FRIDAY									
	SATURDAY									

TOTAL HOURS

REGULAR

OVERTIME

PAY RATE

REGULAR

OVERTIME

TOTAL PAY

REGULAR

OVERTIME

DATE OF PAYMENT

GROSS PAY $

TIME SHEET

EMPLOYEE

ID NUMBER

NAME

ADDRESS

DEPARTMENT

SUPERVISOR

COMPANY

NAME

ADDRESS

PHONE

PAY PERIOD BEGINNING

WEEK ONE

DATE	DAY OF THE WEEK	CLOCK IN	BREAK 1 BEGINS	BREAK 1 ENDS	LUNCH BEGINS	LUNCH ENDS	BREAK 2 BEGINS	BREAK 2 ENDS	CLOCK OUT	DAILY HOURS
	SUNDAY									
	MONDAY									
	TUESDAY									
	WEDNESDAY									
	THURSDAY									
	FRIDAY									
	SATURDAY									

WEEK TWO

DATE	DAY OF THE WEEK	CLOCK IN	BREAK 1 BEGINS	BREAK 1 ENDS	LUNCH BEGINS	LUNCH ENDS	BREAK 2 BEGINS	BREAK 2 ENDS	CLOCK OUT	DAILY HOURS
	SUNDAY									
	MONDAY									
	TUESDAY									
	WEDNESDAY									
	THURSDAY									
	FRIDAY									
	SATURDAY									

TOTAL HOURS

REGULAR

OVERTIME

PAY RATE

REGULAR

OVERTIME

TOTAL PAY

REGULAR

OVERTIME

DATE OF PAYMENT

GROSS PAY $

TIME SHEET

EMPLOYEE

ID NUMBER

NAME

ADDRESS

DEPARTMENT

SUPERVISOR

COMPANY

NAME

ADDRESS

PHONE

PAY PERIOD BEGINNING

WEEK ONE

DATE	DAY OF THE WEEK	CLOCK IN	BREAK 1 BEGINS	BREAK 1 ENDS	LUNCH BEGINS	LUNCH ENDS	BREAK 2 BEGINS	BREAK 2 ENDS	CLOCK OUT	DAILY HOURS
	SUNDAY									
	MONDAY									
	TUESDAY									
	WEDNESDAY									
	THURSDAY									
	FRIDAY									
	SATURDAY									

WEEK TWO

DATE	DAY OF THE WEEK	CLOCK IN	BREAK 1 BEGINS	BREAK 1 ENDS	LUNCH BEGINS	LUNCH ENDS	BREAK 2 BEGINS	BREAK 2 ENDS	CLOCK OUT	DAILY HOURS
	SUNDAY									
	MONDAY									
	TUESDAY									
	WEDNESDAY									
	THURSDAY									
	FRIDAY									
	SATURDAY									

TOTAL HOURS | PAY RATE | TOTAL PAY

TOTAL HOURS		PAY RATE		TOTAL PAY	
REGULAR		REGULAR		REGULAR	
OVERTIME		OVERTIME		OVERTIME	

DATE OF PAYMENT			GROSS PAY	$

TIME SHEET

EMPLOYEE

ID NUMBER

NAME

ADDRESS

DEPARTMENT

SUPERVISOR

COMPANY

NAME

ADDRESS

PHONE

PAY PERIOD BEGINNING

WEEK ONE

DATE	DAY OF THE WEEK	CLOCK IN	BREAK 1 BEGINS	BREAK 1 ENDS	LUNCH BEGINS	LUNCH ENDS	BREAK 2 BEGINS	BREAK 2 ENDS	CLOCK OUT	DAILY HOURS
	SUNDAY									
	MONDAY									
	TUESDAY									
	WEDNESDAY									
	THURSDAY									
	FRIDAY									
	SATURDAY									

WEEK TWO

DATE	DAY OF THE WEEK	CLOCK IN	BREAK 1 BEGINS	BREAK 1 ENDS	LUNCH BEGINS	LUNCH ENDS	BREAK 2 BEGINS	BREAK 2 ENDS	CLOCK OUT	DAILY HOURS
	SUNDAY									
	MONDAY									
	TUESDAY									
	WEDNESDAY									
	THURSDAY									
	FRIDAY									
	SATURDAY									

TOTAL HOURS		PAY RATE		TOTAL PAY	
REGULAR		REGULAR		REGULAR	
OVERTIME		OVERTIME		OVERTIME	
DATE OF PAYMENT				GROSS PAY	$

TIME SHEET

EMPLOYEE

ID NUMBER

NAME

ADDRESS

DEPARTMENT

SUPERVISOR

COMPANY

NAME

ADDRESS

PHONE

PAY PERIOD BEGINNING

WEEK ONE

DATE	DAY OF THE WEEK	CLOCK IN	BREAK 1 BEGINS	BREAK 1 ENDS	LUNCH BEGINS	LUNCH ENDS	BREAK 2 BEGINS	BREAK 2 ENDS	CLOCK OUT	DAILY HOURS
	SUNDAY									
	MONDAY									
	TUESDAY									
	WEDNESDAY									
	THURSDAY									
	FRIDAY									
	SATURDAY									

WEEK TWO

DATE	DAY OF THE WEEK	CLOCK IN	BREAK 1 BEGINS	BREAK 1 ENDS	LUNCH BEGINS	LUNCH ENDS	BREAK 2 BEGINS	BREAK 2 ENDS	CLOCK OUT	DAILY HOURS
	SUNDAY									
	MONDAY									
	TUESDAY									
	WEDNESDAY									
	THURSDAY									
	FRIDAY									
	SATURDAY									

TOTAL HOURS

REGULAR

OVERTIME

PAY RATE

REGULAR

OVERTIME

TOTAL PAY

REGULAR

OVERTIME

DATE OF PAYMENT

GROSS PAY $

TIME SHEET

EMPLOYEE

ID NUMBER	
NAME	
ADDRESS	
DEPARTMENT	
SUPERVISOR	

COMPANY

NAME	
ADDRESS	
PHONE	
PAY PERIOD BEGINNING	

WEEK ONE

DATE	DAY OF THE WEEK	CLOCK IN	BREAK 1 BEGINS	BREAK 1 ENDS	LUNCH BEGINS	LUNCH ENDS	BREAK 2 BEGINS	BREAK 2 ENDS	CLOCK OUT	DAILY HOURS
	SUNDAY									
	MONDAY									
	TUESDAY									
	WEDNESDAY									
	THURSDAY									
	FRIDAY									
	SATURDAY									

WEEK TWO

DATE	DAY OF THE WEEK	CLOCK IN	BREAK 1 BEGINS	BREAK 1 ENDS	LUNCH BEGINS	LUNCH ENDS	BREAK 2 BEGINS	BREAK 2 ENDS	CLOCK OUT	DAILY HOURS
	SUNDAY									
	MONDAY									
	TUESDAY									
	WEDNESDAY									
	THURSDAY									
	FRIDAY									
	SATURDAY									

TOTAL HOURS		PAY RATE		TOTAL PAY	
REGULAR		REGULAR		REGULAR	
OVERTIME		OVERTIME		OVERTIME	

DATE OF PAYMENT			GROSS PAY	$

TIME SHEET

EMPLOYEE

ID NUMBER

NAME

ADDRESS

DEPARTMENT

SUPERVISOR

COMPANY

NAME

ADDRESS

PHONE

PAY PERIOD BEGINNING

WEEK ONE

DATE	DAY OF THE WEEK	CLOCK IN	BREAK 1 BEGINS	BREAK 1 ENDS	LUNCH BEGINS	LUNCH ENDS	BREAK 2 BEGINS	BREAK 2 ENDS	CLOCK OUT	DAILY HOURS
	SUNDAY									
	MONDAY									
	TUESDAY									
	WEDNESDAY									
	THURSDAY									
	FRIDAY									
	SATURDAY									

WEEK TWO

DATE	DAY OF THE WEEK	CLOCK IN	BREAK 1 BEGINS	BREAK 1 ENDS	LUNCH BEGINS	LUNCH ENDS	BREAK 2 BEGINS	BREAK 2 ENDS	CLOCK OUT	DAILY HOURS
	SUNDAY									
	MONDAY									
	TUESDAY									
	WEDNESDAY									
	THURSDAY									
	FRIDAY									
	SATURDAY									

TOTAL HOURS
REGULAR

OVERTIME

PAY RATE
REGULAR

OVERTIME

TOTAL PAY
REGULAR

OVERTIME

| DATE OF PAYMENT | | | GROSS PAY | $ |

TIME SHEET

EMPLOYEE

ID NUMBER

NAME

ADDRESS

DEPARTMENT

SUPERVISOR

COMPANY

NAME

ADDRESS

PHONE

PAY PERIOD BEGINNING

WEEK ONE

DATE	DAY OF THE WEEK	CLOCK IN	BREAK 1 BEGINS	BREAK 1 ENDS	LUNCH BEGINS	LUNCH ENDS	BREAK 2 BEGINS	BREAK 2 ENDS	CLOCK OUT	DAILY HOURS
	SUNDAY									
	MONDAY									
	TUESDAY									
	WEDNESDAY									
	THURSDAY									
	FRIDAY									
	SATURDAY									

WEEK TWO

DATE	DAY OF THE WEEK	CLOCK IN	BREAK 1 BEGINS	BREAK 1 ENDS	LUNCH BEGINS	LUNCH ENDS	BREAK 2 BEGINS	BREAK 2 ENDS	CLOCK OUT	DAILY HOURS
	SUNDAY									
	MONDAY									
	TUESDAY									
	WEDNESDAY									
	THURSDAY									
	FRIDAY									
	SATURDAY									

TOTAL HOURS		PAY RATE		TOTAL PAY	
REGULAR		REGULAR		REGULAR	
OVERTIME		OVERTIME		OVERTIME	
DATE OF PAYMENT				GROSS PAY	$

TIME SHEET

EMPLOYEE

ID NUMBER

NAME

ADDRESS

DEPARTMENT

SUPERVISOR

COMPANY

NAME

ADDRESS

PHONE

PAY PERIOD BEGINNING

WEEK ONE

DATE	DAY OF THE WEEK	CLOCK IN	BREAK 1 BEGINS	BREAK 1 ENDS	LUNCH BEGINS	LUNCH ENDS	BREAK 2 BEGINS	BREAK 2 ENDS	CLOCK OUT	DAILY HOURS
	SUNDAY									
	MONDAY									
	TUESDAY									
	WEDNESDAY									
	THURSDAY									
	FRIDAY									
	SATURDAY									

WEEK TWO

DATE	DAY OF THE WEEK	CLOCK IN	BREAK 1 BEGINS	BREAK 1 ENDS	LUNCH BEGINS	LUNCH ENDS	BREAK 2 BEGINS	BREAK 2 ENDS	CLOCK OUT	DAILY HOURS
	SUNDAY									
	MONDAY									
	TUESDAY									
	WEDNESDAY									
	THURSDAY									
	FRIDAY									
	SATURDAY									

TOTAL HOURS

REGULAR

OVERTIME

PAY RATE

REGULAR

OVERTIME

TOTAL PAY

REGULAR

OVERTIME

DATE OF PAYMENT		GROSS PAY	$

TIME SHEET

<table>
<tr><td colspan="2">EMPLOYEE</td><td colspan="2">COMPANY</td></tr>
<tr><td>ID NUMBER</td><td></td><td>NAME</td><td></td></tr>
<tr><td>NAME</td><td></td><td></td><td></td></tr>
<tr><td>ADDRESS</td><td></td><td>ADDRESS</td><td></td></tr>
<tr><td></td><td></td><td></td><td></td></tr>
<tr><td>DEPARTMENT</td><td></td><td>PHONE</td><td></td></tr>
<tr><td>SUPERVISOR</td><td></td><td>PAY PERIOD BEGINNING</td><td></td></tr>
</table>

WEEK ONE

DATE	DAY OF THE WEEK	CLOCK IN	BREAK 1 BEGINS	BREAK 1 ENDS	LUNCH BEGINS	LUNCH ENDS	BREAK 2 BEGINS	BREAK 2 ENDS	CLOCK OUT	DAILY HOURS
	SUNDAY									
	MONDAY									
	TUESDAY									
	WEDNESDAY									
	THURSDAY									
	FRIDAY									
	SATURDAY									

WEEK TWO

DATE	DAY OF THE WEEK	CLOCK IN	BREAK 1 BEGINS	BREAK 1 ENDS	LUNCH BEGINS	LUNCH ENDS	BREAK 2 BEGINS	BREAK 2 ENDS	CLOCK OUT	DAILY HOURS
	SUNDAY									
	MONDAY									
	TUESDAY									
	WEDNESDAY									
	THURSDAY									
	FRIDAY									
	SATURDAY									

TOTAL HOURS		PAY RATE		TOTAL PAY	
REGULAR		REGULAR		REGULAR	
OVERTIME		OVERTIME		OVERTIME	
DATE OF PAYMENT				GROSS PAY	$

TIME SHEET

EMPLOYEE

ID NUMBER

NAME

ADDRESS

DEPARTMENT

SUPERVISOR

COMPANY

NAME

ADDRESS

PHONE

PAY PERIOD BEGINNING

WEEK ONE

DATE	DAY OF THE WEEK	CLOCK IN	BREAK 1 BEGINS	BREAK 1 ENDS	LUNCH BEGINS	LUNCH ENDS	BREAK 2 BEGINS	BREAK 2 ENDS	CLOCK OUT	DAILY HOURS
	SUNDAY									
	MONDAY									
	TUESDAY									
	WEDNESDAY									
	THURSDAY									
	FRIDAY									
	SATURDAY									

WEEK TWO

DATE	DAY OF THE WEEK	CLOCK IN	BREAK 1 BEGINS	BREAK 1 ENDS	LUNCH BEGINS	LUNCH ENDS	BREAK 2 BEGINS	BREAK 2 ENDS	CLOCK OUT	DAILY HOURS
	SUNDAY									
	MONDAY									
	TUESDAY									
	WEDNESDAY									
	THURSDAY									
	FRIDAY									
	SATURDAY									

TOTAL HOURS

REGULAR

OVERTIME

PAY RATE

REGULAR

OVERTIME

TOTAL PAY

REGULAR

OVERTIME

DATE OF PAYMENT

GROSS PAY $

TIME SHEET

EMPLOYEE

ID NUMBER

NAME

ADDRESS

DEPARTMENT

SUPERVISOR

COMPANY

NAME

ADDRESS

PHONE

PAY PERIOD BEGINNING

WEEK ONE

DATE	DAY OF THE WEEK	CLOCK IN	BREAK 1 BEGINS	BREAK 1 ENDS	LUNCH BEGINS	LUNCH ENDS	BREAK 2 BEGINS	BREAK 2 ENDS	CLOCK OUT	DAILY HOURS
	SUNDAY									
	MONDAY									
	TUESDAY									
	WEDNESDAY									
	THURSDAY									
	FRIDAY									
	SATURDAY									

WEEK TWO

DATE	DAY OF THE WEEK	CLOCK IN	BREAK 1 BEGINS	BREAK 1 ENDS	LUNCH BEGINS	LUNCH ENDS	BREAK 2 BEGINS	BREAK 2 ENDS	CLOCK OUT	DAILY HOURS
	SUNDAY									
	MONDAY									
	TUESDAY									
	WEDNESDAY									
	THURSDAY									
	FRIDAY									
	SATURDAY									

TOTAL HOURS		PAY RATE		TOTAL PAY	
REGULAR		REGULAR		REGULAR	
OVERTIME		OVERTIME		OVERTIME	
DATE OF PAYMENT				GROSS PAY	$

www.ingramcontent.com/pod-product-compliance
Lightning Source LLC
Chambersburg PA
CBHW051759200326
41597CB00025B/4616